INGE'S STORY

JUDITH G. ZALESNE

ON THE COVER

When Inge rang her little bell to signal class was about to begin, we adult-education students eagerly took our seats, anticipating another inspiring session with our beloved teacher.

ACKNOWLEDGMENTS

Thanks to the pandemic (*I can't believe I just wrote that!*) I have spent the last 18 months committed to a project of love: writing about the life of a woman I am blessed to have known — literature professor Inge Probstein. I had written briefly about Inge after her death years ago, mainly for my equally devoted literature classmates, but I had never delved fully, unconditionally, into all Inge's notes and papers.

Undertaking the venture this time, I was fortunate to have the invaluable critiquing of my writing group. Thank you — **Sybil Terres Gilmar, Susan Chamberlain, Reba Parker**, and **Lori Vogt**. It was Sybil, recognizing the extensive hours each of us would be sequestered, who encouraged us to launch into our respective major projects.

Thank you, draft readers **Debbie Goldman, Kinney Zalesne**, and **Dr. Peter Kowey**, for your thoughtful suggestions; if I didn't comply with them all, I value your valid insights. Thank you, **Dr. Ruth Fischer** and **Dr. Barbara Kardon**, for your responses to questions concerning your respective professional expertise, and thank you to the very helpful researchers in the libraries of both **Agnes Scott College** and **Temple University**. Thank you, **Inge Breuers**, for translating from German several original letters and papers. And special thank you, **Carolyn Zalesne**, for your general editing, constructive suggestions, and extremely competent skills in book layout and design; your help has been crucial.

Of course, thank you, **Harvey Zalesne**, for recognizing Inge's story as part of our lives in the last year and a half.

TABLE OF CONTENTS

PART ONE
INGE: HER LIFE, HER CHALLENGES

1.	AN INDELIBLE MEMORY	3
2.	THE KINDERHEIM	6
3.	AN UNEXPECTED MOVE	10
4.	BETTINA STRASSE (BETTINA STREET)	14
5.	NAZI IMPACT	21
6.	RUTH	24
7.	NAZI AUTHORITY	28
8.	IN AMERICA	32
9.	MOTHER AND DAUGHTER: A SEPARATION	37
10.	RADNOR	41
11.	THE "COTTAGE" IN NEWPORT, RHODE ISLAND	46
12.	"FAIRY GODMOTHER" FROM KINDERHEIM	50
13.	AGNES SCOTT COLLEGE	53
14.	YALE UNIVERSITY	64

15. JOB SEARCH, TEACHING (BRIEFLY). THERAPY   72

16. CHARLOTTE. DIFFERENT DIRECTIONS   76

17. RETURN TO EUROPE   79

18. WALKING WITH WORDSWORTH   88

19. NYU MISFORTUNE. "NORMALIZATION"   91

20. TEMPLE UNIVERSITY   98

21. LIFE IS GOOD   103

22. THEN IT ISN'T   111

23. HER POLITICS   119

PART TWO
INGE: MY TEACHER, MY FRIEND

24. CREUTZBURG   127

25. CHOOSING THE SYLLABUS   130

26. THE NATURE OF THE CLASS: AN EXAMPLE (THE SERIOUS AND THE HUMOROUS)   134

27. INGE AND CLASSMATES: A SPECIAL BOND   143

28. LAST DAY OF THE SEMESTER   149

29. INGE'S SUMMER CAMP. THE CLASS' "MINI-REBELLION"   153

30. THE STROKE. THE CLASS WITHOUT INGE   158

31. CROSSLANDS TO BLUE BELL PLACE   164

32. HOW I CAME TO TELL INGE'S STORY   168

INTRODUCTION

For 18 years, I enrolled in Inge Probstein's adult-education literature class. And I wasn't the only one. About 25 of us — mostly gray-haired, retired, decades out of college — repeatedly enrolled to study classical literature with the same teacher, in the same place, on the same day, at the same time. And if Inge were still here, those of us still around would still be immersing ourselves in the pages of Inge's assignments and anticipating our Tuesday mornings with our treasured teacher.

We'd still be seeking Inge's insights on literary characters and circumstances, appreciating her help in recognizing the art in their creation and their relevance to our contemporary times. We'd still be enjoying Inge's wry humor. And an hour-and-a-half after class began, we'd still be mentally exhilarated as we reluctantly left the classroom, our ongoing discussion spilling out the door, onto the porch, down the steps, and onto the driveway and parking lot of the old Victorian house in Radnor, Pennsylvania, called the Creutzburg Center, a township hub for adult-education classes.

Inge brought the classics to life. Assignments ranged from Conrad to Goethe to Stendhal, from Dante to Kafka to Hemingway, from Tolstoy to Mann to Twain, and many others in-between. She proved Italo Calvino's observation: "A classic is a book that has never finished saying what it has to say."

The literature we studied was compelling, but that is not what kept us coming back. Inge was the magnet. We all wanted more of her profound knowledge, her unassuming leadership, her challenging of our own mental probing, her sensitivity, her natural wit, and her genuine respect for — though not necessarily agreement with — every student's perceptions.

My classmates — teachers, physicians, artists, lawyers, homemakers, businesspeople, a librarian, a nuclear engineer, and a diplomat — had either not read these classics in our respective earlier educations or had read them so long ago we relished that deeper understanding filtered through years of life experiences.

Literature and life both tell stories: literature chronicles the broad spectrum of real-life experiences; real-life stories chronicle endless personal feelings and events. For Inge, literature was life, just on another level. It was not separate from who she was. As for her own life, she recognized it as potential literature, a story to be shared. Perhaps that's how she could sustain her surprisingly objective perspective on her own tragedies and troubles. That — plus her sense of humor. What a remarkable combination of wit and wisdom.

Regardless of all the class discussions of human conditions in the books we studied, and their relevance to contemporary life, Inge never talked about her own traumatic family history or personal life — or her own persistent issues with "identity." But all that time, she was writing it down — sometimes in prose, sometimes in poems, sometimes seriously, sometimes humorously. And what a story it was.

Then a stroke felled Inge, and her course came to a halt. Little did I suspect that for me her most challenging assignment was yet to come. It was not a classical literature assignment. It was not even a book in print. Incapacitated and in declining health, Inge could barely communicate, but on one of my visits to her in a rehab/retirement home, she showed me a folder of her accumulated autobiography notes. Summoning up a surprisingly strong whisper, she designated a mission I understood clearly: "This story must be told."

Inge had no living relatives to tell it. Ultimately — and totally unexpectedly — I inherited that folder plus her accumulated lifetime papers. That's when Inge began speaking to me through reams of detailed memories — vivid stories of her German childhood, challenges as an immigrant schoolgirl in America, religious questioning, academic pursuits, personal relationships and trials, and difficult career hurdles. Through her candid comments on issues of religion, education, sexuality and politics, Inge's search for personal identity and respect emerged. We all live with these basic needs, but in Inge's circumstances, perhaps they were more acute.

"This story must be told," she had implored.

This book, Part One, is Inge's story.

This book, Part Two, is my story — the class and the classmates who enrolled in Inge's course semester after semester after semester — for 18 years. It's the story of my very fortunate link to Inge.

Though I knew Inge as her student for all those years, and as a friend after her stroke, how much closer she grew after she was gone — when her own written words made her a compelling presence in my life.

As a curious reader, you'll want to know her story. As her grateful student, I need to share it, not just because my life was immeasurably enriched by her, not just because she wanted this story told, but because reading her own words about her own life will reward you with knowing a woman who faced religious, academic, sexual, and professional challenges — and was sustained by her love of literature and, eventually, her students. You will know a woman for whom words were a foundation, a career, and, fortunately for us, a gift.

PART ONE

INGE:

HER LIFE, HER CHALLENGES

With the triumph of the Nazis, the atmosphere changed quite rapidly.
The first change was that people wouldn't talk ... Silence was soon replaced
by fear, and that is how a whole nation seemingly supported what came to
be a reign of terror and murder that lasted until 1945.
Inge Probstein

Humor is not a mood, but a way of looking at the world.
Ludwig Wittgenstein

CHAPTER I

AN INDELIBLE MEMORY

Near Lubeck, Germany, 1932, ten-year-old Inge was strolling home from school with her friend, Elfreide, when a commotion in front of an apartment house distracted them. The girls stopped abruptly.

"There were two rows of storm troopers in the center, standing with linked hands, legs spread apart, with leather shoulder straps and guns. They were silent. Some of the other people talked in whispers to each other. Elfreide and I stood with the crowd. After a long time, the door of the apartment house opened and a man and a woman and two children were led out [by] another group of SA men with leather straps dangling in their hands. The crowd started hissing. Elfreide was hissing too, and I think I almost joined her. For a moment I wanted to be the same as all the people around me, to be one with Elfreide, and not to let anyone see I was silent. They might think I was Jewish. I might be taken off in the SA truck with the Jewish family right away.

"I don't remember what Elfreide and I said to each other the rest of the way home. I don't know whether she knew my father was Jewish. I had found out about it only a week or two before. I had come home crying because while I was walking across the Opera Platz, a boy threw an empty seltzer bottle at me and called me a 'Judenkind.' I demanded an explanation. That's when my mother told me that my father was Jewish.

"There was always an undercurrent of concern and worry about the political future of Germany. My parents talked about it at dinner; my schoolmates, although we were only ten or twelve years old, discussed it at recess and before and after school." Inge wrote of seeing political parties demonstrate every Sunday: both the Communists and the National Socialists held rallies. "First the Communists, then the Nazis paraded ... bands playing, songs more shouted than sung, in full parade uniform – the Communists in blue shirts and red bandana ties, the Nazis in brown — the SA uniforms ... carrying banners, fighting, yelling, and throwing stones ... the two groups beating each other up in extended fist fights ...

"What was the difference between these two parties? I did not know. I feared both."

Adult German citizens inevitably began to recognize how all those strident politicians were affecting their daily lives, but did they realize the effect of this political turmoil on children?

"The night before the January '33 election, which put Hitler in power," admitted Inge, "I dreamed that his followers, the Nazis, were torturing all the people to death. On the way to school I read that Hitler had won the election. When I got to school I told my schoolmates of the dream, only I changed it around and said I dreamed it was the Communists who were killing everyone. That way it was now a safe dream to relate.

"Well, that was the first time in my life that I lied from my innermost depths and with total cunning. I wanted so much the approval of my classmates, who, I supposed had all turned pro-Hitler overnight. The sad truth is that after that election either all the German people really approved of Hitler, or, like me, they prized the approval of their friends and acquaintances more than their own feelings, whatever they were. For many adults, free expression of their feelings, if they were at all critical of Hitler, would mean the loss of their jobs. So everybody shut up ... With the triumph of the Nazis, the atmosphere changed quite rapidly. The first change was that people wouldn't talk. A grim ... lip silence pervaded in

4

my school and among [my neighbors] … for several months … Silence was soon replaced by fear, and that is how a whole nation seemingly supported what came to be a reign of terror and murder that lasted until 1945."

Amelie and her children: Hans (6), Ruth (11), baby Inge

CHAPTER 2

THE KINDERHEIM

Despite her family's — and all of Germany's — concern about the country roiling from one emergency to the next, Inge's notes of her childhood also reflect many normal, happy times. She recalled hiking in nearby mountains with her family, crossing the frozen river to visit the Christmas market, and coming home to enjoy freshly baked rolls and cheese and local cider. Even when her father suffered a brief mental breakdown, and Inge, three-and-a-half, was sent to The Kinderheim, a small boarding school run by German Jewish educator Anna Essinger, Inge seemed to handle her new situation well. Her brother, Hansl, six years older, went to The Kinderheim also; her sister, Ruth, 11 years older, stayed home. Inge and Hansl (known as Hans) remained students there for a few years, and, despite her young age, Inge retained detailed memories.

Anna Essinger ran a unique boarding school. She had finished her education in the United States, earning an M.A. at the University of Wisconsin. While in America she had admired and adopted Quaker attitudes and supported Montessori teaching methods for younger children, in which child development is encouraged through inner-disciplined, self-directed, hands-on, creative activity. On returning to Germany on a Quaker war relief mission, she became headmistress of the Kinderheim in Herrlingen, near Ulm. Officially called the Landschulheim Herrlingen, the school had recently been founded by her sister, Klara; another sister, Paula, a trained nurse, was the school nurse and housekeeper.

Non-denominational and co-ed, the Landschulheim Herrlingen strongly emphasized arts and physical activity. Every day all the children took walks in the woods and had to do some chores around the building. "Mornings we did calisthenics," Inge remembered, "and in winter we learned to ski ... and on Sundays, Tante Paula ... [who] was warm in her love for all the children ... had all of us in her bed to read us fairy tales. I remember particularly her trip with me to Ulm," Inge continued, "where my tonsils were to be removed. She treated me [to a pastry] ... The doctor was not so nice; he just snipped but did not remove the tonsils ... When we had mumps, we were quarantined to the attic." As for eye exams, Inge remembered facetiously, they "consisted of whether you could see over the hill the Ulm Minster, ten miles away." She was referring to the Gothic Lutheran church, with its steeple rising a record 530 feet.

Tante Anna (Essinger) was a strict disciplinarian who insisted her staff not only set an example of "learning, laughing, loving and living," but encourage each child to be curious, inquisitive, and to find things out for him/herself. That was the keynote of her education philosophy: independent critical thinking. No tests and no grades. Teachers assessed each student's development, discussed it with the student, and sent the assessment to the parents in writing. If that school was the source of Inge's mental processing — self-reliance, analytical contemplation, independent discovery — it is responsible for Inge's lifetime method of studying and for her eventual approach to teaching. Even we, Inge's adult-education students in her class many decades later, benefited from Anna Essinger's influence on her.

Inge recalled Kinderheim incidents and emotions, both good and bad, but all as vivid as if a camera had been filming her life and she had frequently reviewed the reels. Good-time memories include pillow fights, games played hiding under tables, helping older students build

7

a music studio over the new gymnasium, a puppet theater, learning about threshing and grinding at an old nearby mill. Bad-time memories include beatings for wetting her bed, fear of an administrator's taunting son, and humiliation for a faulty piano lesson performance, which, despite her embarrassment, previewed Inge's innate restrained humor:

"Although I tested for musical ability, the music teacher, Fraulein Spatz, ... was strict, and when I kept making the same mistake [playing an incorrect F], she held my hands way above the keys, and I grew red-faced ... That ended my career on the piano ... [Later] Tante Anna saved me forever for music by giving me the triangle part in Haydn's 'Toy Symphony.'"

Hans

Whereas Inge could find humor in describing some of her negative experiences at the Kinderheim, her brother, Hans, evidently disdained almost everything at the school. A six-page hand-written letter from a school administrator to their mother, Amelie Probstein, details Hans' unacceptable behavior, including:

"...he had a fight with Mrs. E. It was a trivial issue...and Hansl became very abusive ...We had a meeting ...and we had to tell him behavior like that is not acceptable and if he didn't change he would have to leave. . .

"We are asking ourselves if it wouldn't be better for Hansl to leave here. It is with a heavy heart to let a young man go and let him find his place in life. It is especially difficult for us because we think that the big city is like poison for him — emotionally, mentally, and psychological [sic]. Because *he is only too ready to take everything in negatively and feeds his attitude toward life with it.*

"It is so important that he faces reality. He should ask himself if maybe he interprets things the wrong way and fights the wrong fights …

"Please try not to tell Hansl he has to stay here. Nobody but Hansl himself should determine this. You can only hope that Hansl comes to this conclusion all by himself."

*Yours,
Anny Wilker*

Other incidents in Inge's notes about Hans, from his childhood all the way to his death sometime in the mid-1990's, suggest a problematic personality. Inge may have kept this long letter among her papers because it reveals an innate, intensely negative disposition. According to notes entitled "My Brother," which Inge wrote years later, when she was a college professor, Hans had been sent to the Landschulheim Herrlingen originally because, as her mother had told her, her father had announced, "Either he or I must go. We cannot live under one roof." Once Hans was sent there, Inge followed. She remembered that when they were children "He was my great hero and solace. I looked up mightily to him." When the family's finances began running low, and their parents could no longer support two children in boarding school, Hans stayed.

CHAPTER 3

AN UNEXPECTED MOVE

Considering all the staggering challenges and unsettling events Inge encountered in her life, as she took pen in hand and looked back through her years, she was determined to evoke the full record of every image in her extraordinary memory.

While Inge and Hans were both boarders, an epidemic of pneumonia sent the younger children home. Inge's parents, Amelie and Erich, met her at the station in Falkenbergen, where the three got on the tram to return home. But Erich got off alone at Glaubsburg Strasse. Confused, Inge turned to her mother, who stunned her with the news that she and Erich had divorced, and Inge would now live with her mother and sister, Ruth, in a two-room attic in Frau Professor Weissmantel's house.

The double jolt — her parent's divorce and the trauma of not returning to her family home – dumbfounded Inge. Living away at school, Inge had had no clue of problems between her parents. Only about seven years old, she was not yet aware of religious tensions and increasing national anti-Semitism that may have affected her parents' relationship. She had had practically no connection to her paternal grandparents and very little to her maternal grandparents. And she did not know at this time that neither set of grandparents had approved of her parents' mixed-religion marriage. Only when she was a few years older did she learn that "Amelie and Erich had gone to London to get married because such mixed marriages were not recognized by Germany … The Christian partner was looked on as a 'Ressenschande' – a disgrace to the German race, and the children were 'Mischling,' i.e., hybrids, like puppies of a mixed breed union."

Religion had been a conscientiously non-existent subject in Inge's immediate family. Neither Amelie nor Erich followed the religious guidelines of their traditions — Protestant and Jewish, respectively. So with their own children, they had diligently ignored the subject. Of the five family members, only Inge considered herself "religious," not because of beliefs but because of that human need to belong: she wanted to be included with all her girlfriends who attended Lutheran Sunday School, and she convinced her parents to let her go with them. (In "A Question of Identity," an essay written as an adult, Inge noted "I had been baptized in the Lutheran Church.")

In her new two-room, chilly attic home, replete with a heating unit for cooking, Inge slept between her mother and her sister. "For a toilet we had to go through the Frau Professor's kitchen." That winter Inge came down with pneumonia. No medication helped until her father, who visited frequently, insisted on a mustard plaster treatment, at that time considered a conventional medical treatment consisting of rubbing a poultice of mustard seed on the chest of the patient. Writing of this memory, Inge recalled "it caused me to scream until I woke the whole neighborhood." And that memory prompted another: "There was a man," she wrote, "going through the neighborhood, always crying, 'Alles das mir Freude macht ist vorbei. Du hast alles gestolen!'" ["Everything that gives me pleasure is gone. You have stolen the whole thing!"]. Recalled decades after the fact, this seemingly random recollection from this stressful time in her childhood — her parents' divorce, her minimal living conditions, her poor health – is perhaps not so random. Nor, perhaps, was that period of her life so stressful, considering what lay ahead.

Inge was seven when she befriended Frau Weiss, an upbeat widow with several "supposedly clever" cats. (Frau Weiss claimed they used the toilet, not the litter box. Inge hoped to see that happen– but never did.) Frau Weiss' grown daughter, Freidl, was a friend of Inge's aunt, Tante Erika (Amelie's sister). Freidl and Erika had emigrated to America in the early 1930's because, as colleagues in an office near Frankfurt, both had been fired, and with unemployment rampant in Germany, women, especially women over 30, couldn't hope to find new positions.

Frau Weiss, who "always wore the same shapeless brown dress," lived in a small dark apartment, but her amiable personality and warmth toward Inge made her a bright and cheerful good friend. They enjoyed talking and walking together to Frau Weiss' "Schrubsgarten," four blocks away, where Frau Weiss grew potatoes, vegetables, and magnificent dahlias — "purple, white, orange – virtual balls of color." The two some-times sat in the window of Frau Weiss' apartment and looked out on the street of four-story apartment houses, often wondering why the street always seemed empty. One day a young priest in his cassock strode the sidewalk across from their window.

"Do you see that priest?" Frau Weiss asked. "If the Communists win, he and all priests will have their heads cut off." Guileless little Inge absorbed every word from Frau Weiss, who was ordinarily lighthearted and optimistic. Years later, remembering her spirited widow-friend, Inge mocked her own childhood gullibility: "How could I doubt a person with such dahlias and such gifted cats!"

As an adult, Inge allowed her natural humor to override the actual fear she remembered about this childhood incident. It is the preroga-tive of the storyteller, especially one who is prone to self-deprecation, to cast a slanted light on remembered facts. But it is undeniable that the dreadful image of the decapitated priest implanted itself in her young mind that day, and fears of such horror intensified as Nazi power increased.

Moving to different areas of Frankfurt became a fairly frequent event for Inge because Amelie kept trying to find better homes, bigger ones in which she could take in boarders. Inge had no choice but to change schools several times.

"At the first school I attended, Fraulein Moaz ... tended to hit the hand with a ruler until it stung. 'Don't worry,' consoled a stoic classmate, 'it fades away' ... And we had Handarbeit, which meant cross-stitching with red and blue threads ... I hated it all." She soon transferred to Furstenberg Middle Schule, where Fraulein Munch "taught us French by daily recitations ... and history by having us recite what we retained from our homework ... She was strict with our posture, correcting it with her long ruler." Having been academically indoctrinated to learn by "independent critical thinking" at Anna Essinger's Kinderheim, Inge resented and disparaged this kind of education.

Only one school impressed Inge, one in which she was never enrolled: the Elizabethan Schule, which her sister, Ruth, attended. It offered the exciting academic challenge that Inge craved. Named after the mother of Johann Wolfgang von Goethe (1731 – 1808), who was often regarded as Germany's greatest literary figure, this esteemed school was considered a training college for teachers of secondary-school girls.

CHAPTER 4

BETTINA STRASSE
(BETTINA STREET)

In the spring of 1932, a year before the Nazis took over, Amelie's entrepreneurial inclinations moved her and her three children — Ruth, Hans and Inge — into a seven-room, fourth-floor walk-up on Bettina Strasse in Frankfurt's West End, so she could take in several boarders. She needed financial solvency. Inge's notes suggest Erich was not an adequate provider. "According to my mother, [my father] spent his money twice before he earned it."

Herr Filz, owner of a butcher shop several miles away, owned this building, and was therefore their landlord. "For me, a girl of ten, the apartment resembled a circus, not only because all seven rooms opened onto a central entrance hall where our three roomers met to don scarves, umbrellas, gloves, slickers, ... but because each roomer capered independently at his/her unique rhythm." Observing this "circus" floor plan with a keen eye and a curious mind, Inge described the tenants.

Lanky Herr Fritz Vöbel, a late-20's actor with a Barrymore profile who felt he should star in films but never got more than minor roles, "drafted me to ... help him practice his parts, which he was slow to learn. I would read his cue lines, and he would respond – not too readily, I

Inge and her mother, Amelie

thought." He flattered her mother outrageously, persuading her to serve coffee at four o'clock, and soon she was baking sweet Streuselkuchen or Bienenstich. "Herr Vöbel was by far the most assertive and ingratiating roomer of the establishment. Hans and I nicknamed him 'Fifo.'"

In the room next to "Fifo" lived Herr Kaplowitz, a graduate student of stage design. "'Ein EdelKommunist,' my mother told me. (To this day [Inge wrote in parentheses] I don't know just what Edel means in this context, since I thought the Communists did not have degrees of nobility.) Never mind. Herr Koplowitz constructed miniature theaters and helped me stage little dramas with stick figures we fashioned from cardboard and wood."

Fraulein Posen lived next to Herr Koplowitz. In her late 20's, she slept late into the morning and went out in the evening, dressed in gauzy gowns and lots of chiffon scarves, which Amelie often ironed for her. "What her occupation was I do not know," Inge claimed.

Hans, then 16, had the large corner room "with four windows and a parquet floor (my green envy) [sic]." He liked to practice all his wrestling holds on Inge. Claiming she was his "steady adversary and hapless victim" during what Inge called "his adolescent sadistic stage," she would never forget Hans holding her out the windows by her armpits – four stories above ground. "He had learned the wrestling scissors-hold in school and wanted to try it out on me. Painful. He often cut all the lights off in a given room, all to rid me of fear. I did not appreciate the lessons." Hans also convinced Inge to bring him tea every afternoon, when he and his good friend were playing chess in Hans' room or Hans was there alone studying.

They did have peaceful encounters, she assured, when they painted watercolors together, "but that was because he was demonstrably totally my superior."

Her sister, Ruth, 22, had her own room, while Inge and her mother shared a room with daybeds on opposite sides and a large table on which she served afternoon coffee — at Fifo's request. To help with finances in these difficult economic times, Ruth got a job as a cashier at the Schubert Theater. As Inge remembered, the only bonus of Ruth's menial job was "she could get the whole family in for free. She quit when she found out there were rats in the box office."

Not until Inge began recalling Bettina Strasse, years after they lived there, did she realize how hard her mother's life in that boarding house must have been. Cooking, cleaning, washing, shopping – they had no refrigerator, so food had to be purchased from several different markets every day. Her mother also tended the pot-bellied stove in each tenant's room, which required hauling coal up to the fourth floor from the basement and taking the ashes down to a courtyard. "How she had time to be affectionate and understanding to us, her children, which she was, is beyond me now," reflected Inge.

Most Sundays Inge spent with her father, Erich, who often took her biking or hiking. In bad weather they played cards. In spring they visited the forest or the airport or the Nizza Gardens, where tropical plants and palms grew in the German climate. Sometimes they visited the strawberry farm of Agatha, an old family helper from their days in Eschersheim, where Inge was born. "Divorced or not, he was often with us," Inge noted. Sometimes Inge visited her father's house, where Frau Simon, his landlady, treated her well. "But it was horrible that my mother always thought of Frau Simon as her rival." As for politics, Erich was sure Germany would stop the march down this unbelievable path. He was certain the German people would revolt against Hitler's outrageous policies and would soon return to normal.

Just as Inge's own life seemed to be settling into more-or-less comfortable routines, increasing anti-Semitism was unsettling life all around her. Nazi power was starting to overrun neighborhoods, sweeping into schools, spreading into homes, infecting relationships. Nazi triumph began bearing down on Bettina Strasse, and soon anyone who didn't raise his arm and "Heil, Hitler" was labeled "disloyal." A distant relative of Amelie, who lived on the second floor of their apartment building and sometimes invited Inge in for "Himbeersaft," a homemade raspberry juice, let her know she was no longer welcome. Even Amelie's father, who had been only a rare visitor – usually with gooseberries, apricots, and strawberries from his garden — let his daughter and her children know he'd have to "time his visits when he thought right," and he instructed them never to visit him.

The women of a Bettina Strasse apartment house would hang their laundry to dry in the courtyard. Inge remembered hearing them early one morning, "singing songs with gusto about the Judan … Nazi songs they had learned ever so quickly." One song ended with a rousing chorus of "Volk ans Gewahr" ["People, man your guns."] The words of another, which the women repeated lustily, were "Die Kopp rollen; die Judan heulen" [The heads are rolling, the Jews are wailing."] That song triggered and reinforced that fearful image Frau Weiss had posited into Inge's head a few years earlier: the headless priest. To this sensitive little girl, these were terrifying potential pictures of people in her midst.

As part of roomer Fritz Vobel's (aka "Fifo's") training to join the SS (he figured SS status would get him more leading roles in plays), he had to learn to ride horses. When he came home complaining that riding gave him "a sore bottom," Amelie felt sorry for him, and sewed him a pigskin seat for his pants. As a tenant he had become close with the family, but when he became SS, Ruth and Inge decided helping him was totally unnecessary — in fact, unacceptable. He had crossed a line that was not to be crossed. "We never forgave Mother," Inge wrote. Fifo did pass his equestrian test, but was soon informed by the SS that he had to move because "it was unseemly for him to room with a half-Jewish family."

Amelie was well aware that their landlord, Herr Filz, was a Nazi who wanted her family to leave. To give him no excuse to evict them, in case he was looking for one, Amelie and Inge bicycled fifteen miles to pay him on the first of every month, rushing to arrive before noon, his deadline. They couldn't trust the mail because he could claim he'd never received it.

Many years later, Inge wrote about Herr Filz. Evidently his

authoritarian black uniform was still clearly etched in her mind when, as an adult, she composed this poem intended to satirize both Nazi innocence and Freudian psychiatry, with which she was familiar by the time she wrote this:

Herr Filz, a butcher by trade, our landlord
In Frankfurt in the Third Reich 'thirty-three
Joined the SS because it seemed wise
For his butcher shop to expand in size,
To his neighbors it seemed very good
Besides, in his newly-bought entirely black uniform
He felt he was more than some earthly worm.

In his uniform, which was entirely black,
Herr Filz, feeling its authority, went back
Went back to beating his wife and children,
Went about denying their will to life.
But that was only the beginning
In the name of his Fuhrer
He took to further sinning
One day transporting Jews to death camps
Another day beating gypsies. No cramps
For Herr Filz, he did all in the name of the state
And his all-black uniform encapsulated his hate.

In '45, however, Herr Filz had a nervous breakdown,
He went all to pieces. At the time the Allies scrutinized
Every Nazi's feces. Her Filz, most disturbed,
Reported to a German psychiatrist
Who said, "Herr Filz, I know you would rather be dead
But let us look back to your childhood,
Your repressed memories, your unconscious id"
And Herr Filz fastened on his father, who always bid

His boy to wash his hands twenty-two times a day.
"Aha," said the sagacious doctor, now we may
For one thing posit why you became a butcher
You wished instead to dip your hands in blood.

Your beating your wife and children
Was the first violent projection of that,
And your work for the SS reflects the same
Rebellion against your father. He was a slave
To cleanliness; instead you dipped your hands in gore.
And what is more, this tranquilizer I'm about to give
To you, Herr Filz, allow you evermore to live
In great tranquility. You see it's all a question
Of your id's resistance to Father Filz' commands,
And I insist you clear your mind of guilty feelings.
Legions have done what you have done.
It's true they killed over six million
Gypsies, Protestants, Catholics and Jews.
You merely helped them climb into the vans

CHAPTER 5

NAZI IMPACT

In the summer of '33, when Inge had just turned 11, Amelie decided the Bettina Strasse seven-room, fourth-floor apartment was too overwhelming an enterprise for her. Managing her tenants and catering to their individual needs required more time and energy than she wanted to take away from caring for her own children, so she moved the family to a smaller second-floor apartment across the River Main. Their new home, in a recently completed Bauhaus-style development of town houses and just a few apartment buildings, meant Inge would have to go to a new school, Holbein Mittelschule. Hesitant to adjust to new teachers, classes and schoolmates, she was naturally anxious. But fortunately, the move worked well for her, as the new neighbors and the new school seemed oblivious to Hitler's proclamations about race. At least, that was Inge's impression.

In a city-wide track meet, Inge, among the best runners, was so happy to gain recognition among her new classmates that she "actually flirted a bit with Naziism": she went home proudly wearing an oak leaf cluster and swastika badge on her blazer, a decoration that her appalled family "greeted with silent disdain." Another time, after standing in a row of Frankfurt schoolchildren recruited to meet the Fuhrer as he dedicated the first stretch of the Autobahn, Inge came home and announced, "He could not be a bad man. He had a nice smile." She remembered how her family stared at her, at first "with silent regret … for my deplorable political naivete." Then Ruth groaned and slapped Inge's ear. "Ohrfeige!" [slap on the ear], Inge wrote. The adults in her family fully recognized the downward route the German government was taking the country, and Inge may have been aware of it. But she was a young girl in need of both recognition by her new schoolmates and success in her new school's activities. Instinctively, these were this 11-year-old's priorities.

That summer the family heard that their Bettina Strasse former-lodger Fritz Vobel — the actor whose riding pants Amelie had softened with sheepskin, the actor who had joined the SS to get starring roles in the theater — was to appear in the Goethe Festival, dramas performed outdoors in front of the Romer Palace. Inge explained, "The Romer and Goethe were equally dear to Frankfurt, the one as literary luminary, the other as the coronation site of Holy Roman Emperors." Inge's whole family excitedly went to see Fritz perform. "Halfway through Act I," Inge recalled years later, "he came barreling through the stage on a black steed. He was out of site until Act II, on foot, and speaking four or five lines. His could not be called a starring role … My family went home in a somewhat funereal fashion."

Despite her early acceptance by her new classmates in Holbein Mittelschule, as weeks went by Inge recognized everyday life was growing increasingly tense. Sensing the Brown Shirts were becoming more aggressive, she imagined they might come and find her brother's "excellent, truly wicked set of caricatures of Hitler's cabinet," and she feared Hans would be arrested. She had a plan in mind: if the Brown Shirts entered their apartment, she would "seize the cartoons, stash them in my bloomers (yes, I wore bloomers then) and shred them into the toilet. Surely, the SA would allow me to go to the bathroom as an innocent youngster who simply had to 'go.' Fortunately this much feared occasion never arose."

It wasn't long before the Brown Shirts, the SA from across the river, began to patrol the family's new neighborhood. "On national flag

22

days they pounded on the door to protest that we were not flying the swastika flag. My mother, always calm, informed them that we were Jewish and therefore prohibited from flying the flag on any day." From my post-Holocaust perspective, I was surprised to read of Amelie's brashness directly in the face of the SA. But at that time, even though the family saw the Brown Shirts becoming more aggressive, they still didn't fathom the long-term intentions of the Nazis. Nor did most Germans, who went about their daily business disliking many government policies but assuming there would be a limit, and change would be demanded. "My mother defied the SA in her soft and steady way," Inge noted. Even her father, when he came to visit, sometimes "joked in a sort of gallows humor" about the "entire bunch of usurpers" who would soon be overthrown.

In early 1934, an ominous incident focused on clarifying the national situation. A poll required all adults to vote on one question: "Do you approve of what Hitler is doing for Germany?" All Germans were to check off "Yes" or "No." Amelie was the only one in their household qualified to vote, "so we intoned peacefully and repeatedly: 'Mother, you must vote "No" for all of us.'" Amelie went to the polls, voted, and came home. "'Mother, how did you vote?'" we implored."

"'When a Brown Shirt stands at your side,' she murmured, her voice shaking, 'what can you do but vote what he wants.'" Forced to be personally complicit, Amelie's conscience took a hard blow. But that momentous plebiscite soon faded in light of the crisis awaiting the family.

CHAPTER 6

RUTH

Inge admitted that everything about her sister, Ruth, was exciting to her. Beautiful and always well-dressed, Ruth was her idol, the one person to whom she looked for guidance and advice. Very popular among her own age group, Ruth never minded taking her little sister along on dates to fancy coffee shops and cafes. Inge, of course, loved the attention Ruth and her friends showered on her, especially when they taught her to sing the latest "Schlagen," trendy songs from films and cabarets. Inge cherished her relationship with her. "Ruth was my best friend," Inge wrote.

In all the years I knew Inge, I never heard her speak of Ruth — or, for that matter, of anyone in her family.

While recalling one visit to Ruth's school, the Elizabethan Schule, Inge wrote, "my sister went with a boy whose name was Bubi Rogge. Bubi, in German, simply means Junior [his given name was Karl] … they were practically engaged. Bubi, to be sure, was a young Adonis in the German mode: blond, blue-eyed, slim, attractive. But none of this seemed to weigh the least bit on him at all. He was a humanist – gracious, understanding, and a friend to everyone in my family."

Among Inge's papers is a postcard from Bubi to Ruth, written early in their relationship, when Ruth was just 15 years old:

Dear Ruth,

Did you receive my letter? I have good news for you. We are coming home Wednesday night. But it's probably going to be late. So I can only come and see you on Thursday. If the weather here is going to deteriorate, we might even leave on Monday.

Until then best wishes, Bubi

Handwritten postcard from Bubi (Karl) to Ruth.

Inge's family, always mindful of the German claims of racial superiority that guided German politics, accepted Bubi because Ruth loved him, and they recognized his winning personality. As Inge had noted earlier, German government problems had been a topic of conversation at the dinner table as long as she could remember. So Ruth must have been aware of Germany's increasing calls for German citizens to protect the superiority of German blood. If government policy had required her parents, Amelie (Protestant) and Erich (Jewish), to go to London to marry way back in 1911, clearly German officials weren't more open-minded now, in the early '30's. But Ruth and Bubi may have figured that since Ruth's mother was not Jewish, according to Jewish law neither was Ruth. She had been raised by parents who had purposely avoided any connection to religion. And she and Bubi, like every couple in love, believed their love could override all potential obstacles. Two young, intelligent, attractive people in love would not let anything, including politics, matter. Nothing could be more important to each one than each other. Despite Nazi power swelling all around them, they allowed themselves to believe – for as long as they could — that love could prevail over national policy.

Inge's memoir does not go into detail about Ruth's health. It just notes that Ruth had begun suffering stomach ailments that required hospitalization. Inge's lack of diagnosis details might suggest that Ruth's intense emotional and mental anxiety about increasing Nazi pressure on their lives — specifically on her plans for life with Bubi, was causing severe gastric pain. Bubi, her longtime German fiancé, was understandably worried, but not just about Ruth's physical health. Now a dentist, Bubi had joined the SS because his family convinced him that Nazi support was necessary for the success of his practice. Moreover, they persuaded him that because Ruth's father was Jewish, Ruth would be detrimental to his career. Inge felt certain Ruth meant everything to Bubi, but in retrospect she discerned that because his SS connections had provided him with insight into Hitler's unspeakable full intentions, he must have felt compelled to make a wrenching decision. Bubi broke his engagement to Ruth and convinced her she had to leave Germany. He told her he would find a Jewish doctor, not only to treat her immediate health problem, but also to get her out of Germany and safely to Palestine. Inge wrote that she and her family were stunned, devastated.

"He was genuinely troubled," remembered Inge. "He saw the danger of the Nationalist Socialist state more clearly than my family did at the time," she wrote. And because he loved Ruth, and wanted her safely out of the country, "he persuaded my sister that her only chance of survival lay in emigration to Palestine and in [an arranged] marriage to a young Jewish medical doctor who would leave Germany with her for Palestine." Bubi did find a Jewish doctor who was anxious to emigrate, and whom, under these difficult circumstances, Ruth tried to consider seriously. According to Inge, "Ruth had no wish to go to Palestine but was going ahead with the plan reluctantly."

Whether she would have actually left Germany for Palestine can never be known, for Ruth began receiving letters and calls from the family of this Jewish doctor. They let her know they were deeply opposed to Bubi's plan to have her leave with the Jewish doctor because Amelie was not Jewish, and therefore Ruth was a "shiksa," a non-Jewish girl. Rejected by both German gentiles and German Jews, Ruth grew distraught. One afternoon when Inge was outside practicing gymnastics, her mother, having just returned to their apartment, flew outside shrieking. Ruth had closed herself in the kitchen and turned on the gas. Ruth was 23.

"For me," wrote Inge years later, "it was the loss of my world." Besides suffering the tragedy of her beloved sister's death, Inge admitted that she herself felt guilty. "[Ruth] had asked me just the week before, while showering, how I would feel if she were no longer here. And I thought it was a joke. She was cremated, and I had to face the world alone."

CHAPTER 7

NAZI AUTHORITY

As the Nazis tightened their grip, parents of Jewish girls started taking their daughters out of the local school and enrolling them in the Philanthropin, a renowned old school established by the liberal Jewish community in 1804. (Recognized through its long history for its legendary intellectual leadership, the Philanthropin, in a building constructed in 1908, remained in existence until the high school closed in 1941 and the elementary school in 1942.)

"My older brother attended this school," wrote Inge, "but there wasn't enough money to send both of us there, so I tried to get away with being a Christian." In April, 1934, the principal of Inge's public school, who dressed every day in his SA uniform, sent out notices that every girl who wanted to return the following year would have to show her registration card for the Bund deutscher Madel (BDM), the League of German Girls. "To be a member, of course, one had to be an Aryan," noted Inge. Amelie got the message: they had no choice. They had to leave Germany if they could.

"My father and brother decided to stay, my brother to finish his education at the Philanthropin, and my father because he hoped for the end of Hitler. My father thought the German people would come to their senses ... He actually believed still that Hitler would be overthrown in a few months, that the German people were not 'idiotic' enough to tolerate such a regime."

Inge's father, Erich

Amelie had visited relatives in America in pre-Hitler 1928, so she had a valid passport, but "Germans had no interest in helping a half-breed," so getting papers for Inge proved difficult. "My mother pursued every effort to leave Germany and take me with her," and ultimately came up with "a remote connection – my great-grandfather, … [who] had immigrated in the early 19th century from the Austro-Hungarian Empire, from a part of which after World War I became Polish." It was a stretch, but Amelie, desperate and determined, applied to the Polish Consulate in Frankfurt. Eventually, "my American uncle, in Germany with Tante Erika, Mother's sister, for a summer visit, came to the rescue. He took charge, explained his request to the Consul, and placed a flat of Luckies [Lucky Strike cigarettes] on the table." A visa for Inge, he was told, would take three months. "He placed another flat of Luckies on the table, and they said it would now take three days." Inge was given a visa that granted her permission to enter the United States within the next 30 days.

"I said good-bye to Papa on the Old Main bridge," Inge wrote, recalling the spot where she often rode her bike to meet her father. As she remembered their meeting that day, neither wanted to show unusual emotions. Both either believed, or pretended to believe, their separation would not – could not — be final. Neither could tolerate such a thought. "I acted as if this good-bye was only a bit of a good-bye, and my father did likewise." He, determined to keep the conversation normal and upbeat, talked about "how good plums tasted this time of year." When the time came to say "auf Wiedersehen," Inge was traumatized. Her notes explain that that scene at the Old Main bridge continues to replay in her mind, and ever since that heartbreaking moment, she's had difficulty speaking the word "good-bye." The word catches in her throat and sometimes triggers tears. Inge always deeply regretted that this last conversation with her father at the bridge, their special meeting place, was so superficial, but she did not know then she would never see her father again.

Inge and her mother left Germany in the summer of 1934, sailing third-class on the S.S. United States from Hamburg. She had just turned 12 on June 11th. "I was armed by my mother with two expressions in English: 'Thank you' and 'Enough.' My mother felt these words would be indispensable in the ship's dining room. She was correct." Except for a little seasickness in the Irish Channel, Inge found the voyage to be fun. When the Statue of Liberty came into view, Inge, with all the other passengers, ran on deck, cheering in great excitement and anticipation. On seeing Lady Liberty, the exuberant immigrants might have exclaimed exactly what the poet Emma Goldman claimed was her first reaction when she saw the statue: "Ah, there she was, the symbol of hope, of freedom, of opportunity!"

It was only after all the passengers went back to retrieve their belongings that they realized that while they were rejoicing at the sight of New York, some ship stewards were scavenging through their baggage for jewels and cash. "My mother had taken a few pieces of jewelry with her because the amount of currency one could take out of Germany was painfully small." The jewelry was gone, as was Inge's own ten-dollar savings.

Germans had no interest in helping a "half-breed," so Amelie, desperate and determined, applied to the Polish consulate.

CHAPTER 8

IN AMERICA

First- and second-class passengers disembarked and went through normal procedures, but uniformed inspectors instructed Inge and Amelie, third-class passengers, to just wait there on Ellis Island, the "a grim and shabby" crowded immigration station within view of the Statue of Liberty. It was four o'clock on Friday afternoon. No entry officials seemed to care about helping them get through all the required procedures, i.e., standard questions, health check-up. Eventually an administrator told them they'd have to stay at least until Monday, when they could then sign an affidavit assuring authorities that Inge would enroll in school immediately. Luckily, Inge's uncle — that same uncle who fortuitously had been visiting in Germany when Amelie, his sister-in-law, needed help getting herself and Inge out of the country — was in New York to greet their arrival. "Once more, my uncle, who was outraged by the bureaucracy, intervened," and again his interceding succeeded. "Indeed," wrote Inge, "it took less than ten minutes to sign the bond and get out of Ellis Island."

On the ferry from Ellis Island, she wrote, she saw a Negro woman for the first time. She had seen a Negro before, but only once — the man who sold nuts on the street in Frankfurt.

The thrill of landing in America was just slightly diminished by the unbearably hot late August weather, which Inge found exceedingly humid, stifling, and oppressive. Their first stop was Wanamaker's on Broadway at Ninth Street. Primarily a major Philadelphia department store, Wanamaker's at this time had a large New York store as well. Inge bought a "middy" blouse and a dark blue skirt; Amelie bought a dress. "Because of the heat" Inge remembered, "I had to throw up in front of Wanamaker's. I was afraid I'd be arrested and deported."

They stayed a few days with her uncle's relatives in the Bronx, which in 1934, due to cheap rapid transit construction connecting Manhattan years earlier, had grown into neighborhoods of large apartments filled with former residents of crowded Manhattan tenements. Mother and daughter spent those few days sightseeing in Manhattan, where flashing lights on huge marquees lit up movie theaters on Times Square. Much of Rockefeller Center was still under Art Deco construction (its official opening had been just three months earlier), and the 3500-seat Center Theater, on the corner of West 49th Street in the Rockefeller Center complex, had changed from a movie theater to a showcase for live musical ice-skating spectacles. The Empire State Building, just three years old, was a major tourist attraction, and Horn & Hardart automats were popular. Everything that Inge and Amelie saw and did is not recorded, but Inge wrote that she found herself "duly impressed with the glory of New York City."

From there they traveled to Evanston, Illinois, on their way to their goal: St. Paul, Minnesota, where extended family (probably family of the same uncle, husband of Amelie's sister, Erika) resided in a sizable German American community. In Evanston, they stayed with Friedl Weiss, the daughter of Inge's widowed friend, Frau Weiss, of the clever cats and splendid dahlias. Frau Weiss was also visiting her daughter, who had some health problems. Friedl had married an elderly Dutchman, described by Inge as "a fierce ex-intelligence officer" who enjoyed subjecting everyone to "furious quizzes." If he wanted to make Inge uncomfortable, he succeeded. "At breakfast it was my turn to be quizzed on German and European history. Everything I said was totally wrong, and I cried every morning because of my wounded intellect. He demolished everyone else systematically at every meal. We all feared and hated him." Fortunately, Evanston offered Inge more than the hated Dutchman. Friedl Weiss lived just two blocks from Lake Michigan, where Inge loved to swim. A competent athlete, Inge had always been a good swimmer, and she thrived during her days in Evanston. "My delight was the beach and the waves of the lake. I went there every afternoon."

Not long after they moved to Minnesota, Inge heard that both Friedl Weiss and her mother had died. Very upset at that news, Inge questioned her mother. "What happened to them?" she demanded. Amelie outrageously fantasized her response: "Oh, I imagine the Dutchman was after their money and cut their heads off." Immediately Inge thought of the priest in the street she and Frau Weiss had seen years earlier, and that terrible potential image of a decapitated priest Frau Weiss had implanted leapt into her head. As it turned out, what Inge heard was not totally correct. Yes, unfortunately, Friedl had died. Fortunately, Frau Weiss had not. Unfortunately, though, she had returned to Nazi Germany.

Although Inge's helpful uncle graciously hosted Amelie and Inge in St. Paul, three days after they arrived, he confronted Amelie: "What's the matter? You have been here three days, and you haven't found a job yet! This is America! Everybody works in America!" Amelie fully expected to work but was still trying to determine what she could do. Under pressure, she took a job in the home of a Mrs. Davidson, and with Inge she moved into the Davidsons' 12-room apartment on Summit Avenue, a miles-long promenade of Victorian mansions, many of which, after the Depression, were converted into large apartments. Inge's notes claim this area was the "in" place to live in St. Paul. Actually the Davidson family didn't really live there. They lived "far out at one of the lakes and kept the city apartment for occasional visits to the theater or the opera. My mother's functions," wrote Inge, "were to chaperone the adolescent children when they came to the city for an evening," and to serve them dinner as well. Her salary was $25.00 a month ($520.00 in 2022).

Bitter cold winter in St. Paul was wonderful for kids – school yards became skating rinks and parks became ski slopes. But school itself – Inge entered the John H. Webster School in seventh grade – was daunting for a child who spoke no English. "I understood nothing that the teacher said; I understood nothing that my classmates said. I was completely lost. After a few weeks, however, I learned some words and even foolishly volunteered to answer the teacher's questions when no one else would. My classmates laughed hilariously at my mispronunciations [i.e., *Pot'a mac* for Potomac] and my invented grammar … It was on the skating rink and on the ski slopes that I became accepted by my classmates. Here language ceased to separate me as the class dunce."

Everyday life presented challenges for Inge and her mother. In 1934, supermarkets were not yet prevalent. "To shop for food, one had to ask the grocer, naming what one wanted. But what were the names, and how do you pronounce them? My mother and I prepared ourselves for shopping with the German-English lexicon, but often forgot the pronunciation when we were face to face with the grocer.

"What our American friends served when they invited us for lunch was sometimes a delight, sometimes a problem. A big dish of green jello with bits of chicken and vegetables embedded in it captured my amazed enthusiasm, as did a platter of sliced tomatoes festooned with Miracle Whip. What a country!

"Other friends served us mutton chops, a mid-western staple. My mother had told me that when you are a guest, you must eat everything on your plate. I ate every inch of the mutton chop with its large layer of fat and was ill for three days … I have never been able to eat lamb in any form since then."

Together Inge and Amelie enrolled in English language classes at the International Institute of Minnesota, whose mission was to help immigrants and refugees become self-sufficient. Both worked diligently to adjust to their new culture in America. "We met many other immigrants. The classes were excellent, and the friends we made there ended our feelings of isolation." They assumed in time they would finally feel "at home" in St. Paul.

But in early 1935, a letter came from an old family friend, Agatha Graf, who had been the family housekeeper back in Eschersheim, Inge's birthplace, and whose strawberry farm Erich would often take Inge to visit when he'd spend Sunday afternoons with her. Agatha had immigrated to the United States, and was now living in Germantown, a section of Philadelphia, Pennsylvania. When she learned that Amelie and Inge were in the United States, she wrote to them, insisting they come to live there, in her community in The City of Brotherly Love. Enchanted by the promise of these place names – Germantown, City of Brotherly Love — Amelie didn't need more encouragement to leave Minnesota. "My mother and I boarded a Greyhound bus for the trip east. It was minus 32 degrees when we left St. Paul."

CHAPTER 9

MOTHER AND DAUGHTER: A SEPARATION

At first Inge and her mother stayed at the downtown Philadelphia YMCA, but soon moved to the Germantown "Y." Inge enrolled in the Charles W. Henry School, a K-8 public school on the corner of Carpenter Lane and Greene Street, and Amelie searched for full-time work.

"Since she loved to cook and bake," Inge wrote about her mother, "and had no employment history whatever since her marriage in 1911, she leaned on her culinary skills ... and was hired as a second cook" by Mrs. John Dorrance, matriarch of the Campbell Soup Company family, to live and work in their mansion, Woodcrest, on their 120-acre Radnor Township estate on Philadelphia's suburban Main Line. "Then I had to face a new reality, one that I met with tears and unbelief. [My mother and I] would now have to live apart. How could we, who had supported each other in every painful aspect of navigating a country where language and ways were indeed strange? ... I cried torrents."

Reading these notes, I could almost see Inge's crestfallen face reliving that memory. Fortunately, despite its emotional poignancy, unlike the heartbreaking memory of saying good-bye to her father on the Old Main bridge in Frankfurt, this traumatic recollection then allowed Inge a little room for humor — or facetious cynicism. Reading the notes just a bit further, I could then picture Inge smirking as she exaggerated: "the

[Dorrance] house had 175 rooms, 35 servants to keep up the estate and 20-plus on the house staff, but no place for anyone's child." (Actually, the Elizabethan Tudor Revival style three-story mansion has 51 rooms in 47,000 square feet. Designed by Horace Trumbauer, Woodcrest was built in 1901-1903 for James W. Paul, son-in-law of Philadelphia financier Anthony Drexel, on his 238-acre estate. Historically certified in 2008, the Woodcrest mansion is now part of Cabrini University, a Catholic school on 112 acres.)

Despite her sorrow at separating from her mother, Inge, a child well-experienced in facing unwanted challenges, knew she'd have to become resigned to their situation, and ultimately convinced herself "it had to be." She also wrote "we were fortunate in finding a place for me to stay."

Miss Moffett, principal of The Henry School, found a family, the Spahrs, who agreed to accept Inge as a boarder while Amelie worked. An elderly Swiss couple economically affected by the Depression, they were more like grandparents than parents to 12-year-old Inge. "The only inflexible rule that I recall of the Spahr household," remembered Inge, "is that during the 7 o'clock evening broadcast of Lowell Thomas and, following that, of 'Amos 'N Andy,' not one word was to be spoken by anyone. For some time I had the impression that those men were, in fact, the American saints ...

"I had been aware of the Great Depression of the 30's. The long unemployment lines, the strikers, the people selling apples ... the streets in St. Paul seemed only to be the obverse of the German scene in the last years of the Weimar Republic. Now, living with the Spahrs, I saw men coming almost daily at the back door to ask for food. Mrs. Spahr always prepared a sandwich or some other gift of meat or pie for them. Beggars at the door I could not recall from Germany, although poverty there was widespread."

The one person who was especially solicitous in helping Inge adjust to her new world was Miss Moffett. Affectionate and attentive, this caring Henry School principal, according to Inge, paid attention to every child's progress and problems. It is certain she paid attention to Inge. Whenever Inge wrote a little essay, Miss Moffett posted it on the school bulletin board. With Miss Moffett's help and praise, "I made great steps in English, and helped my classmates to solve problems we had before in Germany," Inge wrote, without specifying what kinds of problems they were. Then she added, "In spelling bees, I was a good speller" and Miss Moffett "praised me lavishly." On Fridays Miss Moffett took students to her home near the school, where she read to them [*Mary Poppins*] and they listened to classical music concerts. Evidently Inge was making great strides since her days in a St. Paul school, when she had felt she was "the class dunce." Her natural intelligence may have eventually prevailed even without Miss Moffett's warm and compassionate encouragement, but with it, this shy, tentative foreign student broke through her justifiable apprehension. "That school had an esprit of Brotherly Love," Inge remembered. "I was very happy in this school."

Mother and daughter worked out a plan. Inge saw Amelie "on weekends, when she met me at the Radnor Station, and we took the long walk through the fields and the long walk through the Dorrance estate. On her day off, we would see any Katherine Hepburn movie showing. She was my mother's favorite actress, and we learned to speak English from her. Then we ended the day with a small dinner for 80 cents at Horn & Hardart. Not bad, that. We really enjoyed our times together." Katherine Hepburn was an excellent teacher; Inge spoke English with not even a trace of an accent.

By the late 1930's, when she felt herself to be fairly competent in the English language, she wrote that her "drive to conformity reasserted itself," and she happily joined in activities with kids her age. It was a glorious time for her: she swam at the "Y," hiked with friends on the Wissahickon trails, played kick-the-can and other street games with neighborhood kids "until the fireflies came out and dusk turned to dark," joined the Girl Scouts, and went to Girls Scouts Camp Indian Run, which she loved so much she cried when the summer session ended. She even attended Sunday School at the nearby Presbyterian Church, but only for two weeks, "this because a busy [busy-body?] neighbor had become concerned that I did not go to church or Sunday School. But the Sunday School was, in fact, hopelessly condescending and childish. Our teachers there addressed us as if we were nincompoops. I simply had to quit."

Two comments allude to Inge's experiences in ninth grade at Germantown High School: (1) "I flunked gym because I could not get my locker to serve me [open], and I was therefore too late with [getting on] my gym shorts"; and (2) her Latin teacher thought she was reading *Julius Caesar*, but "I read all of *Gone With the Wind* in Latin class."

Meanwhile, in Germany, Erich's prediction that the German people would come to their senses and oust the despicable Nazi regime proved fatally wrong. Early in 1939, Hans, who had remained a student in the Philathropin, sent notice that Erich had died or been killed – it was never made clear – after being seized and sent to a concentration camp. A few weeks later, Hans, "shell-shocked and shaken" by Erich's death, managed to slip out of Germany on what may have been the last passenger ship to leave before the war. In May of that same year, 1939, the *M.S. St. Louis*, with 937 passengers, mostly Jews trying to escape Nazi Germany, was turned away from both Miami and Cuba. It managed to get some passengers to western European countries, but had to return to Germany; 254 of the forced-to-return passengers ultimately died in concentration camps.

CHAPTER 10

RADNOR

With Hans joining his mother and sister in America, Amelie had to find a place for both children to live. She was able to rent a small house Inge and Hans could share, about a 15-minute walk from the Dorrance property. Located in Wayne, a community in Radnor Township, a western suburb of Philadelphia, their little house rented for $35.00 a month, plus coal and utilities. Amelie's monthly salary was $65.00. "Our lifesaver," wrote Inge, "was that my mother came over every evening with a dinner pail full of the Dorrance leftovers ... (I don't mean she scraped the plates. For heaven's sake 'NO') but it was those Dorrance leftover dinners that eked out our nourishment." This move to Wayne required Inge to again change schools. She left Germantown High School to enroll in Radnor High School.

During the summer, the Dorrances, Amelie's employers, like much of Main Line society, left for Bar Harbor, Maine, and Amelie was required to go with them. So much for Dorrance leftovers. Inge, at 13, felt proud that she managed to feed Hans and herself on $4.00 a week. Years later, when she was writing autobiography notes, she said "I still have the grocery store slips to prove it to myself." Not knowing how her children were managing, and seemingly determined that they must have butter, Amelie sent them butter packed in Killarney Tea tins.

Inge remembered receiving parcels with melted butter seeping through brown paper wrapping.

"Poor as we were in Wayne, it would have helped if my brother could find a job and contribute his wages to the household." Speaking English was not a problem for Hans, who had studied it for years in Germany; he spoke with a British-German accent. But Hans never recovered from what the Nazis had done to his father and to his beloved Germany. He was never able to start over in America, as Inge and Amelie understood they must. He did make one attempt to find a job, wrote Inge. Through The Hebrew Aid Society (now HIAS – Hebrew Immigrant Aid Society, created in 1881 to help immigrants find housing and employment) he found work in a clothing store on Chestnut Street in downtown Philadelphia. Hans showed up at the store ready to work, but when he was told one of his responsibilities would be sweeping the floors, he stormed out, incensed and insulted that he, an educated, intellectual young man with the equivalent of a college degree in Germany, should be required to do such menial tasks.

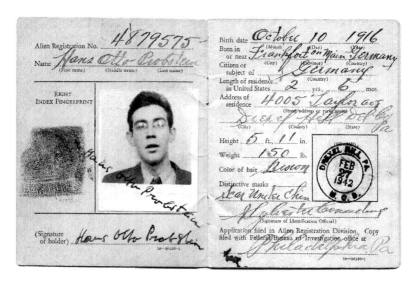

Hans never recovered from what the Nazis had done to his father and his beloved Germany.

"I think that was his undoing," Inge wrote. Hans became increasingly depressed in the following years, requiring ongoing psychiatric help.

In 1939-41, while sister and brother lived together, with no money to spend, they created their own good times. Years later, when recapping these Radnor years together, she wrote of an incident which revealed something significant in herself:

"Hans was very emotional and reached out for my hand once under an apple tree in someone's neglected yard. I was utterly cool, and that is the only time he ever opened himself up and reached out to me for love. I gave none. I was afraid of emotion myself."

When the weather allowed it, they hiked. On weekends, they packed sandwiches and took their sketchbooks and watercolors to "ramble around the countryside (much of Radnor Township was still countryside then) to find good places to paint." Painting, Inge wrote, was her "love" while a student at Radnor High School. This creative gene may have receded and been replaced by other creative inclinations as her life progressed, but it never totally faded. In the last years of her life, painting became her dominant productive outlet.

High school cliques are the norm among teenagers, and Radnor High School fit the pattern. But Inge understood that most of her classmates had been together since kindergarten, so she, a newcomer, rationalized her "outsider" status. "Yet, many of them were, as individuals, my friends," she noted, clearly appreciating those classmates who accepted her. I don't know whether they knew she had tragically lost her adoring and adored sister to Nazi values, and her beloved father to Nazi rule, or whether they were aware she had been forced to leave her native homeland, then had to separate from her mother and board alone in a strange family's home for the previous few years. I don't know if they knew she had been compelled to adapt to a new culture and to attend school in America before she could even speak or understand English.

After facing all these trials, an adolescent girl understandably might have not adjusted, might have wanted to retreat into a shell. Perhaps Inge's core strength instructed her not to succumb; perhaps these tragedies and challenges actually strengthened her resolve. Whatever kept Inge going, whatever kept her connecting to life around her, she knew she had to adjust, and she complied.

Wanting to belong, feeling connected to others, being part of an identifiable group is a natural inclination, especially among teenagers who, consciously or sub-consciously, often value "belonging" as part of their self-worth. Despite the extraordinary traumas of Inge's young life, that natural inclination still motivated her. She recognized her "outsider" status, but possibly because of an exceptional need to belong, she began to "[go] around with a bunch of would-be Bohemians, but in essence, simply a 'fast' group of boys. We got into a few scrapes drinking beer at the Conestoga Inn and driving recklessly. My first sexual experience with one of these boys was so awkward and unpleasant, I'd like to forget it, but I do remember it whenever I see his face in the Radnor yearbook of '41." Whether that specific experience had a more significant, long-term effect on Inge's sexual preference is questionable. According to Freud, one cause of homosexuality can be a distressing heterosexual experience, in which "the libido changes over to an inverted sexual object after a distressing experience with a normal one." Her other notes, up to this point, show no indication Inge considered herself homosexual.

Besides enjoying making a few friends at Radnor, Inge was impressed with many Radnor High School teachers. Having earned M.A.'s and Ph.D's, they were qualified to teach in colleges and universities, but the Depression had precluded them from finding appropriate teaching positions. Radnor students benefited, Inge wrote, for these teachers shared their love for their respective academic fields with their students. Inge rated most of them as "excellent." Even so, she noted, "I dropped Latin because I could only giggle at the instructor." Was he inept? Was he odd? Was he funny? No explanation offered. "But I loved the English classes," she raved, "especially Mr. Stabley's, and I had much pleasure from Miss Meyers and Mr. Stall, with whom I visited the World's Fair," which opened in 1939 in Flushing Meadows, Queens, New York. Planned to coincide with the celebration of the

44

150th anniversary of George Washington's inauguration, the real intention of "The World of Tomorrow" was to raise the spirits of Americans after the Depression. Inge thrilled at the seven-foot robot that had a vocabulary of 700 words and could smoke, and she marveled at the pavilions exhibiting new inventions — automatic washing machines, air-conditioning, color photography, nylon stockings. At the heart of the Fair she surveyed "Democracity" — a miniature model of a utopian city of the future.

Typing class was also on her Radnor roster, as her notes explain: "They played music during typing class, and when the music repeated the same note three times, I automatically repeated the same key three times. I flunked."

Overall, Inge's good memories of her Radnor High School days included participating in many clubs and swimming in nearby Martin's Dam. As for classmates, many years later she wrote that more than being defined by cliques, "the real division ... was between the academic [college bound] and commercial [employment bound] students ... It persisted, as I noticed, even at our 50-year reunion."

CHAPTER II

THE "COTTAGE"
IN NEWPORT, RHODE ISLAND

During the summer between her junior and senior years of high school, Inge decided she could help alleviate her mother's very tight budget. "[M]oney was scarce at home, and I believed there were better places to spend the summer than Wayne, Pa. ... I hired myself out as a parlor maid to a Chestnut Hill matron, Mrs. D., who was used to spending her summers at her French chateau, which, in 1940, along with most of France, was occupied by Hitler's armies." With her seasonal routine interrupted, Mrs. D. "was forced to make do for the summer by renting a large waterfront mansion – probably called a 'cottage' – on Narragansett Bay," while Mr. D., who suffered from severe arthritis, remained in Chestnut Hill for the summer. In the Cadillac limousine drive to Rhode Island, along with the butler/chauffeur, Mrs. D., and Mrs. D.'s five spaniels, Inge had her first lesson in appropriate parlor-maid deportment. "I had addressed Mrs. D. as 'you.' The chauffeur corrected me. Mrs. D. was to be addressed solely as 'Madame' ... in the third person singular. It was not too difficult a lesson to remember. Fortunately, the five spaniels answered to 'you.'" It seemed to Inge that "Madame felt that World War II had been incited to thwart her habit of spending five months of every year in the Loire, staffed by civilized servants who knew how to serve an American woman and her retinue of guests properly … She deplored the loss of her French servants, who were perfect in every respect."

Inge's salary was $30.00 a month, plus room and board. Other servants were a German couple, Marie (cook) and Karl (butler/chauffeur); Rose, a "diplomatically silent," young, tiny Italian kitchen maid; and "my aunt, whose official title was private secretary to Madame but who shared the upstairs work – cleaning bedrooms and baths – with me." (Inge's notes never mention a relative in America other than "Aunt Erika" and her husband, who hosted them in Minnesota. I am assuming this mention of "my aunt" refers to the same Aunt Erika.) Inge explained that ordinarily a parlor maid's responsibility is to help the butler serve the family tea every afternoon and three meals a day, arrange salad, do the dishes, and set the table. But Madame often entertained ten or twelve for lunch and fifteen to eighteen for dinner. So at breakfast, Inge had to carry trays to the rooms of Madame's many house guests. Neither a parlor maid nor a private secretary was supposed to have "upstairs duties," but in 1940 many servants had to double up on duties because so many regular domestic workers had left to find better paying jobs in defense industries.

Two servants were problematic to Inge: Karl and Marie, the butler/cook couple. They were ardent Nazis. Inge said nothing of her father and of her own connections to, and feelings about, Nazis, but when the daily news announced ever more frequent and severe German bombing raids over London, and Karl and Marie rejoiced, Inge cringed. Every day Karl predicted the total destruction of England and gloated over an expected German victory by September. Inge kept quiet, but in recalling that stressful situation, she remembered she "usually fermented inside, but tried to keep still while we servants ate our meals in the back dining room." Despite her feelings about the Nazi couple, Inge noted that "we ate very well indeed in the servants' dining room, for Marie cooked and served the same food for us as for the 'Herrschaft' [ruler, authority]. The summer of 1940 was my introduction to crème brûlée and lobster thermidor."

During rare, free on-duty time, Inge went to the servants' dining room to read. "I wasn't always doing high falutin' reading, but one afternoon I sought to elevate my mind with Kant's *Critique of Pure Reason*, of which I'm sure I understood little, when Madame appeared with a guest to whom she was showing the house. She asked me, condescendingly, as was her manner, what I was reading. When I mentioned Kant, it did not seem to sit well with her. She probably thought it would be *Reader's Digest*. It is indeed curious that after that day she determined that in my no-commitment 'on-duty' hours, I was to iron table linens."

The garden around this mansion overlooking Narragansett Bay was neglected, except for a profusion of hedge roses. Once, "when Madame was giving a large party, she decided to save on the florist's bill and asked me to fill the vases with these tiny roses. I arranged about 15 vases … but she was repelled. 'Did you think I was giving a baby party?' she demanded. 'Throw all these roses out and call the florist to see what they can do in an emergency' … We had no flowers for that party."

Inge's days working for Mrs. D. were long. She began at 7 a.m. by "de-hairing" the carpeted stairs of hair shed by the five spaniels. At 10 p.m. she was finished, as long as the dinner dishes were dried and put away, and she'd walked the dogs up and down the driveway several times. In her one hour off in the afternoon, she had to shower in the one bathroom all the servants shared, and "change from my morning uniform ("blue and white narrow-striped outfit with white apron *sans bib*) into my afternoon uniform of burgundy silk moiré with my frilly laced cap and apron … Whenever the doorbell rang, I had to grab another white apron *with* a bib just to see who was there."

No one was less suited for a "frilly laced cap" than Inge, with her short straight hair; her thin, agile, athletic body; her plain though pleasant features; her down-to-earth demeanor. And she was no more suited for this menial job than for the "frilly laced cap," but she was pragmatic and responsible. There she was — a teenager faced with unfortunate life circumstances so far, but a teenager accepting those circumstances while seeming to astutely observe herself in the situations she faced, almost as an outsider monitoring her life while living it. So when Mrs. D. "tested" Inge every day by scattering a specific number of hairpins throughout the house after breakfast, especially under furniture, and then checking the mantel each evening, where she had told Inge to place the hairpins, to see if Inge had cleaned thoroughly enough to have retrieved the correct number, Inge diligently performed the duties required of her, while mentally accumulating the remarkable — and sometimes absurd — stories she was living.

CHAPTER 12

"FAIRY GODMOTHER" FROM KINDERHEIM

Back in Radnor for her senior year, Inge had no plans other than to get a job after graduation. She would love to have planned for college, as most of her classmates were doing, but economically that was not a viable choice. Then, "one fine Saturday, a woman came to call at our decrepit little house. She was a Mrs. Tugendreich, sent from our erstwhile boarding school." Inge was referring to the Kinderheim/Landschulheim Herrlingen of Inge's early childhood in Germany. In 1933 Anne Essinger had exiled the school, now renamed Bunce Court, to Kent, England. "She [Mrs. Tugendreich] had been sent to find out what had happened to my brother and me. Now working for the Friends Service Committee, she was not about to see any obstacle to my going to college. The administrative communications and connections of the Quakers got into action," and with their help, plus that of a Presbyterian minister, Inge was granted a four-year-scholarship to Agnes Scott College in Decatur, Georgia, a Presbyterian-affiliated, liberal arts college for women, located within the broad boundaries of metro-Atlanta, Georgia.

Mrs. Tugendreich seemed to appear out of nowhere, a fairy godmother alighting her magic wand on Inge and literally changing the direction of her life. If fate in the form of Nazis had ended Inge's happy childhood in despair and sorrow, uprooting her from her homeland, now fate in the form of an unknown, caring Quaker was opening doors to unforeseen opportunity. Inge, Hans, and Amelie were stunned – and ecstatic.

Mrs. Tugendreich had not appeared out of nowhere. Links going way back to Inge in the Kinderheim boarding school, the Landschulheim Herrlingen, had brought her to find Inge. As Inge's notes explain, the boarding school, "now exiled in England" brought them together. It was the school's Quaker principles that Anna Essinger, original headmistress, had instilled into the boarding school's philosophy, keeping its ongoing staff caring about former students, even, if necessary, connecting to Friends Service Committee in America.* Thus, Mrs. Tugendreich's arrival in Radnor, Pennsylvania.

*During the war, Anna Essinger established a reception camp for hundreds of German children sent to England on Kindertransports. By the time Essinger closed Bunce Court in 1948, she had taught and cared for over 900 children, most of whom called her Tante ("Aunt") Anna. She remained in close contact with some former pupils until she died in 1960.

During the summer following graduation from Radnor High School, Inge volunteered at a New Hampshire Friends Seminar for refugees who had escaped from a French concentration camp.

"I met Erwin there," she wrote. "He was my first boyfriend, and often we went swimming in what I now believe was Golden Pond." One memory of a harebrained incident in New Hampshire probably had Inge smiling as she wrote it. She and another participant in the Friends Seminar, a former rector of a Polish university, were assigned to sweep the grass and leaves from the floor of the group's meeting place, a church. Instead of sweeping them out the door, "[w]e swept them into the register on the floor. You can imagine our embarrassment when the next Sunday, [as the air vents went on] the leaves and grass all at once arose."

CHAPTER 13

AGNES SCOTT COLLEGE

In September Inge was off to college on the Silver Meteor train from Philadelphia to Georgia and Agnes Scott College. "How my family managed sending me off to college is more than I can understand even now. The train fare alone amounted to about half of my mother's monthly salary. Also, I must have had to buy a few things – an alarm clock, a bedspread, possibly some items of clothing, an army trunk. I had no winter coat my first year in college, only a raincoat, but in Georgia, the winters were less severe than in the North."

Her memory of her first view of Atlanta was the profusion of signs in the train station: "Black" and "White." She had not been aware that segregation was such an entrenched and enforced part of life in Atlanta. According to her notes, "The streetcar conductors had guns to enforce the practice of seating." That this absolute segregation was an acceptable way of life stunned Inge.

The main building on the 90-acre Agnes Scott campus was an Italian Renaissance Revival style mansion built in 1905-06, when Agnes Scott Institute (originally Decatur Female Seminary, founded 1889) became Agnes Scott College. One rule of the college, which Inge knew before she arrived, but which she chose to ignore, was "No Smoking," so her addiction created an immediate conflict. "On the first day, I could not obey smoking rules, and had a cigarette in a Boy Scouts haven, and afterwards traveled miles on a bicycle to have my cigarette."

Inge and her assigned roommate, Virginia Carter, got along very well. Just weeks into the first semester, Inge learned from Virginia that before the girls arrived for their freshman year, the college had called Virginia's parents to notify them — in fact, to ask if they minded – that Virginia would room with someone named Inge Probstein. What the school was really asking was if the Carters minded that Virginia's roommate was Jewish, which they surmised, though incorrectly, was accurate. Virginia and Inge remained roommates — and academic rivals — for the rest of their college years. "In our standing," Inge wrote in her memoir, "she got the first prize and I got the second." (Reading about Virginia Carter in Inge's papers, I realized this was the same Virginia who called me several months after Inge's stroke to learn where Inge was recovering. I do not know who had given her my name or phone number, but it was clear she was deeply concerned about Inge and was desperate to reach her, which, I assume, she did.)

One line in Inge's college memories says "Wendy, my classmate, had a momentous influence on me. She is still my best friend." Because Inge did not indicate the dates on which she wrote her autobiographical notes, I do not know what "still" means. But the handwriting of these particular memories is more unsteady than most of the other handwritten accounts, so this was probably written late in her life.

Pearl Harbor, December 7, 1941, required some emergency changes at Agnes Scott College, i.e., local government took over some dormitories for use by troops. While other students had to scatter to find housing, Inge did not. She had become a favorite of the dean, Miss Scandretti, who invited her to stay in her home. It was this same dean who sat by Inge's side when she was in the infirmary recovering from an appendectomy in her junior year, and again when she was quarantined with measles.

The war initiated other ripple effects. In 1943, wartime concerns about scarce provisions as well as uncertain help availability required a change in meal service in the dining hall of the Agnes Scott main house. Instead of being served at cloth-covered tables by African American waiters, students lined up in cafeteria style for breakfast and lunch, while dinner remained family style, served by uniformed waiters. Inge befriended the head waiter, Thomas, who, she was amazed to learn, earned $4.50 a week, and she wrote of her friendship with Klebee, a maid for students and faculty. Inge's notes include her own distress when Klebee would not sit down at a table with white people. Inge also remembered that at one point in her years at Agnes Scott College, when "the Negroes went on strike," she volunteered to help in the kitchen, an offer that startled her classmates. "Some girls were shocked. They had to clean their own quarters, and they wouldn't volunteer to serve." Inge was surprised by their reaction to her offer to help. Four years in Georgia never acclimated Inge to inherent Southern prejudice and attitudes of white supremacy.

Inge knew she was lucky to have received a full scholarship, which had come, she wrote, through the help of "a Presbyterian minister born of Jewish parents in Jerusalem, who had converted in a Christian college in Turkey, I believe." He assured her of financial aid from both Protestant funds and a group called Children of Israel Refugee Relief Committee. Though she recognized her literal half-Christian half-Jewish status, she did not commit to either religion. And that created a problem at this Presbyterian school, especially during Religious Emphasis Week.

During her first two years in college, "When all the others stood up in chapel to signify their rededication to Christ, I alone remained in my seat ... It was agony. I felt like an outcast and tried to slide down in my seat so that no one would notice. Of course, they did, and merely thought me an unrepentant sinner. My friends made appointments for me with the visiting minister, telling [me] only after they had set the hour and the place, that I was to receive special help to resolve my doubts." Neither that minister nor others offering "spiritual counsel" considered her half-Jewish background, though one gave her a copy of the New

Testament, "which through cross-references and bold-face type, showed how the Gospel bore out the prophesies of the Old Testament." That was an old lesson to Inge, one she had learned in those Lutheran Sunday School classes she had convinced her parents to let her attend with her childhood friends. What she was seeking now, according to her notes, was more than a scriptural relationship between Judaism and Christianity.

She could have chosen not to attend chapel during Religious Emphasis Week. Jewish students were excused, but Inge did not consider herself Jewish. She had never been to a Jewish service — or even to a synagogue, until her Jewish classmates invited her to attend a service with them. After that service she spoke with the old rabbi, who was "appalled at my lack of religious training. With a Jewish father, what was I doing attending synagogue for the first time at the age of 18? He did not seem interested in the fact that I was half something else."

If forced to identify one's religion at Agnes Scott, which she felt was the case, Inge leaned towards Christianity, a remnant of her childhood Sunday School lessons.

According to an article in the March 9, 1943, edition of *The Atlanta Constitution*, Inge was among the 165 college students — all committed Christians — from 11 different foreign countries and 12 different Georgia institutions at the meeting of the Baptist Student Union Council of Atlanta. After the whole group sang "America," the leader gave the students an opportunity to express themselves. Inge, then a sophomore, was the first to raise her hand, but it was not Christianity on her mind. It was democracy:

"Democracy is something to be fought for. We had a chance at democracy in Germany, but we didn't fight hard enough for it, and then this man Hitler came along, and see what my country has today. We must and will win this war, and then we must continue to work for democracy here and everywhere."

The tension of expressing her religious — or non-religious — identity wore on her. "As a junior and senior in college I stood up among the ranks in chapel. Perhaps my motives were similar to those that made me want to join the crowd in Germany." She was referring back to the time she and her young friend, Elfriede, saw a crowd at the door of an apartment house waiting to see soldiers take away a Jewish family — just a week or two after she'd be called "Judenkind" and learned she was half Jewish. That was "when I wished to be like everyone else," Inge wrote, "and not be singled out. But now, in college, it was with some weariness that I stood, tired of being a sore thumb."

Classes challenged Inge, but she thrived on academic challenge. In English I, she wrote papers on George Eliot and Jane Austen, for which she received the grade "Merit." She had no idea whether that grade equaled an A or B or C; she just accepted that designation as "satisfactory." In writing her memoir, she remembered that in her first readings of these English novels she disliked *Pride and Prejudice*. "I didn't realize it was supposed to be funny. The lack was in me. I had no sense of humor!"

No sense of humor? Inge? For students who knew Inge in our adult-education literature classes decades later, that is an astonishing statement. It may very well have been a typically self-deprecating notation. I believe students at Agnes Scott College must have known Inge's dry humor. A newspaper clipping from *Agnes Scott News*, Wednesday, May 3, 1944, includes another student writer's interview with Inge. In a column entitled "The Tattler," Inge recalled her early years at the Kinderheim, revealing her ever-present subtle sense of humor:

Sew What?

Why, potholders, of course. Also sox, scarves, and nightgowns. If you don't know how, ask Inge, who, growing confidential over a cup of coffee, talked about her grammar school days, when she used to ply the needle. In the first grade she knitted potholders. In the second, she crocheted potholders. In the third, she cut holes in

sox and scarves and then darned them with blue and red thread.
The next year she made a nightgown with a white ruffle. In the
fifth grade, alas, she was forced, and I quote "to repeat the night-
gown," as she forgot the year before and sewed up the neck and
sleeves. The bell rang before sixth grade struggles could be revealed.

Evidently, that hatred of *Handerbeit*, her elementary school's requirement to learn handiwork, which she had mentioned in her Kinderheim memories, still rankled her in college, where it then fed her sense of humor.

How, when, and where, did she develop that quiet wit which captivated her college friends, later endeared her to adult colleagues, and delighted our adult education class? Perhaps her gifted sense of humor was innate but understandably suppressed during traumatic times. Evidence of it surfaced in her descriptions of her mother's tenants in their seven-room Bettina Strasse apartment, in her memory of Frau Weiss' extraordinary cats, and in other recollections. Or perhaps accounts of distressing events justifiably nurtured her cynicism, which then grew into the wit, the humor, that infused much of her mature writing. But many of her memories describing Agnes Scott College are mostly straightforward, i.e., her history teacher taught everything from the British standpoint; her geometry teacher, expecting more of her, dismissed her until she could meet the requisite college level; and all the women faculty were addressed as Miss or Mrs., though some had doctoral degrees.

Inge enthusiastically took advantage of extra-curricular opportunities. A champion swimmer on the school team, she managed to include time in the pool every day. She expanded her love of music by attending concerts in Atlanta as well as on campus. In her junior year she helped design the sets for a prize-winning show, an original production satirizing life and personalities at Agnes Scott, performed by the junior class at the end of traditional Black Cat Week. She became editor of *The Aurora*, the college magazine, and she wrote for the school newspaper, both outlets to release her wry humor.

Speaking before the Atlanta Rotary Club in 1942, she revealed her understated humor and keen perception. Her topic: "Why I Like Americans." (See pages 60-61.)

Speech to Atlanta Rotary Club, 1942
Reprinted in Coca-Cola Magazine, 1942 (?)

Why I Like Americans!

by INGE PROBSTEIN

A College Student of German Ancestry
Finds Us Full of Ideas and Plans

EDITOR'S NOTE: *Born in Frankfort, Germany in 1922, Inge Probstein came to the United States in 1934, with her mother, who is a naturalized American citizen.*

Finishing high school in Wayne, Pennsylvania, Miss Probstein entered Agnes Scott College as a freshman in 1941. During her freshman year she stood second in scholarship.

Her hobbies are: horseback riding, swimming, and dramatics.

☆　　　☆　　　☆

I HAD my first contact with Americans in a railway station in Frankfort, Germany, where I lived before I came to the United States. One day I met an American couple there, and this couple was eating oysters—two dozen of them to be exact. The price of oysters in Germany was prohibitive (something like 22 marks a dozen which in foreign exchange was worth less than $7.00, but to the average German it meant almost the equivalent of $22.00). Since I had never seen an American couple before, nor even an oyster, and seldom that much money at one time, the effect of seeing all three at once was positively revolutionary. And consequently, whenever I thought of Americans in the future I associated them with oysters and much money.

I had two other ideas about Americans—their use of safety-pins and their non-use of cooking utensils. My sewing teacher had told me that American women do not sew their hems, rather they pin them up with safety pins. This appealed to me, for I hated sewing with a passion, and that day I decided that I should like to live in America.

What I heard about American cookery had the same appeal. It seemed perfectly reasonable—in fact, it was the one practicable solution to the pot-and-pan washing problem—to heat everything in its respective can, serve, and season to taste. I *knew* that I should like America.

Though the ideas I had of Americans were limited and pitiful enough, the average American's picture of a German is not much more complete and reasonable. Americans are perfectly exasperated with me if I fail to fit in one of three classifications they have devised for the German "type". But when it turns out that the FBI is not hunting me any more than the Gestapo, when people find that I am fond of neither beer nor sauerkraut, and that my father did not wear short leather pants with embroidered suspenders—that he did not even *yodel*—what chance have I of seeming genuine?

It is a misfortune that we nations know so little of one another. Though I would not blame you for having little desire to know the Germans better *now,* I, for one, am glad I came to know the Americans.

I like Americans! I like them for two big reasons. First, they are honest, and second, they are full of ideas.

When I say that Americans are honest, I mean it in a broad sense. Americans are honest with themselves, which, after all, is the highest type of honesty. Europeans pretend in so many ways to be *super* human. Their exaggerated reserve, their love of titles, (the longer the better) their insistence on "form", are all evidences of a striving to cover up the human element in man and to supplant it with a detestable and troublesome formalism—why, I don't know.

What a relief to know one's neighbor, as an Englishman who spoke to us at school recently remarked. Not that your neighbor's business is any of yours. But we humans are naturally curious about each other, and in Europe that

27

"Why I like Americans" Page 1

60

curiosity is looked down upon as "meddling" and "snooping."

When you travel on a train in Europe you are shut up in a little cage, called a compartment. This keeps you safe from the other travelers and vice versa. How much you miss by traveling in this manner! I have met fascinating people on trains. There was the woman who sat next to me on the "Southerner" when I came to school in September. I could write a volume on her, and another one on the green grocer from Spartanburg — with lots of words to spare.

There is a self-consciousness in European people that I have never felt here. As a child in Germany I was conscious of the very color of the socks I wore Sundays. When their color was not white, mother would say, "Even the chickens will laugh at you." Not that my mother is abnormal; the saying is merely a German proverb in good standing and much in use. I like Americans because they leave a wide margin for social errors of such nature. I have seen children wear *red* socks on Sunday here, and the world did not tremble.

I like Americans because they do not deify man. The German father comes home and tells the family "where to get off"—probably because that is the best tonic for his ego. He is on a hallowed pedestal from which he will never be asked to dismount and " . . . come, help me do the dishes, honey." I may be mistaken about all this, but I have seen *pictures* in magazines of husbands helping with the dishes and pushing baby carriages in parks. And we Germans are taught to believe in the truth of the printed page.

My second big reason for liking Americans is that they are full of ideas. Probably one of the causes of the European dilemma today is a starvation of ideas that promised a reasonable degree of success. America, as far as I know, has never undergone such a period of cynicism as did Europe in the 20's and 30's. Hitler triumphed in Germany partly because he was the one man with an idea in which he firmly believed.

But in America everyone has ideas. I read a book recently which describes America's crucial period of the 30's. The author spoke of the interested response of the people to Roosevelt's recovery plans; how in that time thousands of letters came pouring into the White House every day from farmers, school teachers, men in industry—who had developed individual master schemes for national recovery and "licking" the depression. In America everyone has plans; the church, and labor, and business men. Every respectable ladies' sewing circle has a plan for world reconstruction, and usually a firm conviction that *its* plan is *the* plan.

People have plans for trade agreements and preventing a post-war depression. They have plans for international cooperation and a lasting, really lasting, peace. Americans have stood a supreme test during the past year. Even in the face of the highest tax rate in American history they have managed to emerge with a plan for reduction of the public debt. A European would have shrugged his shoulders in despair long ago and blamed God for the bad state of things in general.

I think that in that very fruition of ideas and plans that want carrying out lies the safeguard of American democracy. Under no other form of government could as many diverse plans have the chance of development they enjoy here. America furnishes proof that groups with different plans can live together harmoniously and work for the ultimate good of all.

28

"Why I like Americans" Page 2

Feeling brazen one day in their senior year, Inge and her friends went swimming without their swimsuits. They were caught, causing an uproar. "Dr. McCain [president of Agnes Scott College] said our scholarships were now canceled, and we had to pay him for the four years. This was impossible." The actual punishment became denial of Mortar Board and Phi Beta Kappa recognition (to which they had already been named) until the spring semester. "So came graduation, and I won a scholarship to Yale."

Despite the scholarship, Inge had to earn her own spending money, so the summer before enrolling in Yale University's Graduate School of Arts and Sciences, she got a job in a pottery store on Chestnut Street in Philadelphia. Her boss, she thought, was an unreasonable man whom she saw fire employees for trivial reasons. He promised to pay Inge an hourly wage if she'd come in early to empty the kilns, and Inge, needing every penny she could earn, accepted his offer. When he refused to pay her appropriately, and Inge reminded him of his promise, he shrugged, insisting, "Do you have it in writing?"

Next she found employment packing cookies at the Nabisco plant in Philadelphia. Her description of herself in an assembly-line scenario evokes Inge as Lucille Ball in a classic "I Love Lucy" episode: "When I came 'on line' the forelady ordered me to the line making cardboard boxes ... from flat cardboard. Every box I tried to make popped open hopelessly, and after 1 hour of my total failure, the forelady yelled at me, 'What's the matter with you ... [you] can't even do a single box!'

"I was crestfallen. The forelady then moved me to the 'Pride Assortment' line of cookies on the endless belt. There were dozens of such lines, all packing a different NABISCO cookie. "On my line you had a stack of pleated waxed cups on your right hand, a trayful of stacked cookies on your left. Your job was to combine the two at the rate of 70 per minute, placing them in a particular space ... for your particular piece of the 'Pride Assortment.' This was not too difficult, but it became grim and monotonous very quickly. Then, too, the waxed paper cups cut your fingers, which began to bleed. There were signs on every pillar that you must report to the infirmary at the first sign of such laceration, but there was absolutely no one to take your place in the line, so what could you do?" Lucille Ball indeed!

Later that same summer Inge had a job briefly at Human Engineering on Delancey Street in Philadelphia. "It paid $15.00 a week, but I learned a lot," she wrote. According to Merriam-Webster Dictionary, human engineering is "the management of industrial labor, especially with regard to relationships between people and machines." The company tested all sorts of human activity to improve people's use of industrial machines. (Too bad they hadn't checked Inge's assembly-line job at Nabisco, where she had been in dire need of help!) Human Engineering sent Inge to Wanamaker's department store in downtown Philadelphia to "count the people who used their left hand, and those who used their right, to get off the [escalator]." The store detective "thought I was a spy and had me arrested," and Human Engineering had to come to her rescue.

CHAPTER 14

YALE UNIVERSITY

Writing about her graduate studies, Inge started with "Yale was, above all, terribly frightening." She entered graduate school in September, 1945, when Yale College was still a male bastion.

Although a woman was first awarded a Yale Ph.D back in 1894, and the number of female graduate students had started increasing in the first decades of the 1900's, when Inge moved to New Haven, the number of women graduate students seeking Ph.D's had declined significantly. The reasons are not clear, but researchers of Yale history suggest some possibilities: many women had sought graduate degrees in order to teach at women's colleges, but women's colleges were beginning to favor male faculty; women were choosing to marry and raise families; and American immersion in WWII in the early 40's affected decisions by potential women graduate students. Whatever the reason, when Inge arrived, women on the Yale campus were minimal, and possibly not always welcome. Years later, even after Yale College became co-ed in 1968, some faculty attitudes toward women lagged considerably. An early undergraduate coed remembered her Introductory Economics professor saying, "he couldn't imagine why we [women] were there, and he couldn't imagine that we had anything to contribute. So he wasn't going to call on us. And he never did."

It is understandable that in 1945 Inge found the Yale environment "frightening," or at least uncomfortable. She remembered being one of forty-two women [was that her humorous exaggeration?] living in a former fraternity house, St. Elmo, intended for twelve boys. And, as she recalled, neither of the two bathrooms had a lock on the door or a curtain around the tub. At least the small room assigned to Inge had a window; it looked out onto a Catholic church.

As for her classes, "I had Old English every day," she recounted. "Mr. Manner taught in the old manner. He frightened us every day ... In addition, I had Tucker Brooke, who taught us pre-Elizabethan drama and passed me in Latin because it was medieval Latin, the story taught by Chaucer (the man in the pear tree)." Evidently Inge already knew that story well, so translating was less difficult. But "Mr. Brooke committed suicide and left no trace that I had passed, so I had to pass it once more. My favorite teacher was Gordon Haight, who taught a course in the novel.

"In all, women were restricted, and there was nothing to do about it... The year passed, and I received a prize, the Tew Prize, for having the best record of the graduate school, which," she added, "meant a hundred books to buy." The Mary Cady Tew Prize was awarded for exceptional ability in philosophy, literature, ethics, or history during the first year of graduate study. The prize was books.

A "Missing" Memory from College Days

At this point in her memoir, Inge wrote, "All this time I left out a great step I took with Ellen Douglass Leyburn. I did not know what Shakespeare meant by 'possess.' She did, and it led to her bed to stay." Inge was referring to her Agnes Scott College days, where Ellen Douglass Leyburn was a revered instructor of English. A 1927 Agnes Scott alumna, Leyburn had earned an M.A. from Radcliffe College in 1928 and a Ph.D. from Yale University in 1934, and then had returned to teach at her undergraduate alma mater, where, in 1957, she was named head of the English department. At some point in Inge's time on campus, 1941-45, Inge spent a week with Leyburn and recalled, "I was radiant now, and all the love made me happy." Their relationship continued for years after Inge graduated, mainly dictated by the academic calendar: at Christmas Inge would meet Ellen in New York, where they enjoyed theater productions and fine restaurants, and during parts of the summer vacations, Inge would stay with Ellen in Georgia.

One of the intellectual attractions linking Inge and Ellen must have been their shared appreciation of literary satire, often a means of expressing humor in its many forms, i.e., irony, wit, sarcasm, allegory, as in Inge's use of "possess" in the paragraph above. (See Shakespeare: *Richard II*, Act III, Sc. 1). Many years later (1978) Yale University Press published Leyburn's book, *Satiric Allegory*: Mirror of Man, a study of satire in Jonathan Swift's *Gulliver's Travels* and Samuel Butler's *Erewhon* (Note: *Erewhon* is *"Nowhere"* almost spelled backwards.) Among Inge's Yale papers is "The Name and Nature of Nonsense," her 20-page analysis of humor in Lewis Carroll's *Alice's Adventures in Wonderland* and *Through the Looking Glass*, a universally recognized satire. Among the attractions that connected the two women must have been their shared joy in a similar sense of literary cleverness and common sense.

Alice in Wonderland: "Nonsense for Nonsense's Sake"

Inge's paper, "The Name and Nature of Nonsense," is a serious contrast of nonsense (silliness) and "logical nonsense" (wit and puns). Inge appreciated both. Literary critics have looked at this Lewis Carroll work through lenses of imagination, politics, and philosophy. It is a humorous but sober satire of the Victorian age: Alice appears in fantasy Wonderland, where she meets (British) imperialism and superiority, (British) justice via an inflexible King and Queen of Hearts, and (British) culture adamantly defending its own particular education system, manners, and etiquette. The satire is palpable. So is the wit.

But Inge took a unique approach — that is, plain nonsense can be enjoyed just for its own absurdity. "The effort to find sustained satire or systematic allegory in the Alice books," she wrote, "is due to a failure to appreciate nonsense for nonsense's sake." Then choosing to concentrate on Lewis Carroll's clever choice of words, she explained that wit requires a thought process that inevitably makes a point. In support of her own appreciation of nonsense, Inge noted that Alice Liddell, the second of three young sisters who begged Reverend Charles Dodgson (alias Lewis Carroll) to make up a story while he rowed them on the Thames, urged him to be inventive. "There may be nonsense in it," seven-year-old Alice encouraged Reverend Dodgson, giving him permission, as well as imploring him, when his storytelling slowed down, to keep creating the story — even if it's nonsense.

As a student years later in Inge's adult education literature classes, I admired the basic humor in her personality, but until I learned of her study of *Alice in Wonderland* and *Through the Looking Glass*, I hadn't realized her deep-seated delight in obvious silliness. I should have, because, though a brilliant and erudite teacher of literature, Inge had fun writing her own silly nonsense poems for our adult education class, sometimes ending weeks of profound literary discussion with "nonsense" summaries of it all. Perhaps Inge's appreciation of Lewis Carroll's frivolity in writing nonsense words inspired her own delight in writing nonsense poems — obviously just for the fun of light-hearted nonsense.

But Inge also analyzed deeper implications and interactions of sense and nonsense in Lewis Carroll's extended fantasy. She explored in detail the humor of the *Alice* characters, concluding that "if Carroll has evolved a philosophy of sense and nonsense, it is the White Knight, rather than Alice, who embodies the Carrollian Weltanschauung [world view]." In *Through the Looking Glass*, the White Knight, who keeps falling off his horse, repeatedly tries to create practical ideas. Unfortunately, they turn out impractical, upside down. But he is well-meaning, and he cares about Alice and wants to help her. Inge summarized her perception of the White Knight story:

"… [O]ne ought, in any event, be prepared to see the world of sense upside-down, for who can say how long upside can remain up and downside will stay down? Who can reestablish order when reason itself begins to turn back somersaults with the course of the world? Nonsense, or the ability to think with one's feet in the air, is a healthy counterbalance against the potential absurdity of all reasonable things."

Nonsense? Yes. But reading these words in Inge's "Through the Looking Glass" paper made me think of Inge's indelible memories of her childhood in Nazi Germany and of her optimistic father, who believed the German people would come to their senses. What was in her mind, I wondered, when she wrote "who can say how long upside can remain up and downside will stay down? Who can reestablish order when reason itself begins to turn back somersaults with the course of the world?"

In an annotated *Alice in Wonderland*, American theologian Reinhold Niebuhr states: "We preserve our sanity by laughing at life's absurdities, but laughter turns to bitterness and derision if directed toward deeper irrationalities of evil and death." I believe Inge understood Niebuhr well.

What were Inge's insights in reading Lewis Carroll's White Knight satire? As with all literature, what a reader personally brings to it impacts what that reader takes from it. I read and re-read Inge's paper on Lewis Carroll's work, and found myself compelled to think about what was churning in Inge's mind when she wrote that conclusion: "Who can reestablish order when reason itself begins to turn back somersaults with the course of the world?"

Her notes made me wonder about Inge's gift of irony: did the tragedies she faced growing up initiate a sharp sense of absurdity, which developed into her attentiveness to humor and ultimately into her own acute wit? Or, despite the tragedies of her childhood and trials of her early teens, did an innate sense of humor mature into her keen, intellectual wit? According to psychiatrist Dr. Ruth S. Fischer, victims of tragedy will respond however they can, i.e., deny, despair, minimize, *satirize* — depending on that person's particular strengths, weaknesses, life experiences and social situations. "Satire can be a coping mechanism, ... a high level of coping mechanism," Dr. Fischer adds, "indicating strength in dealing with the self and the world."

Whatever instincts and influences affected Inge's sharp and often ironic perception of world situations — from her own tragic experiences of life's irrational absurdities, to her ongoing shared emotional and intellectual insights with Ellen Douglass Leyburn, to her intense Yale studies of irony in literature — her wit expanded into a strong attribute of her personality and her teaching. More than 35 years after earning her Ph.D., our class of serious adult literature students were enjoying the power of her wit, and re-enrolling year after year. (*Alice in Wonderland* and *Through the Looking Glass* were in our syllabus.)

Boswell

Among Inge's Yale papers is her doctoral thesis: *"Boswell's London Journal of 1778."* Why did she choose to write about this 18th-century Scottish diarist, the biographer of the essayist/literary critic Samuel Johnson? Her notes do not answer that question, but it is worth citing that during Inge's graduate studies at Yale, Frederick A. Pottle, the renowned editor of James Boswell's London Journal, 1762-1763, published in 1950, was the Yale Sterling Professor of English. Inge was awarded her Ph.D. in 1951. Undoubtedly Professor Pottle influenced her, but probably in support of Inge's own strong attraction to Boswell's work. According to Professor Pottle, Boswell's "zest for life was not fully savored until all was written." Considering Inge's extensive autobiographical notes, I understand her rapport with Professor Pottle's insight.

I believe Inge also "fully savored" her deeply embedded life experiences by entrusting them to paper. Her need to record them was an ongoing commitment during her entire adult life; she started scripting her life story several times — sometimes in ink, sometimes in pencil, sometimes on loose leaf paper, sometimes on yellow tablets, sometimes jotting down clear anecdotal recollections, sometimes expounding in pages of fully developed accounts, sometimes concentrating specific personal reactions into poetic forms, most times in tiny but fluid handwriting, sometimes in self-forced scrawl. With no presumption of associating the personal narrative of the famous, well-born, 18th-century Scottish Boswell with the autobiographic reflections of the 20th-century German immigrant-child-turned-English-literature-professor, I recognize both writers as meticulous observers of their own lives and life around them, and I believe Inge's need to tell her story found compelling encouragement in the candor, strong sense of dialogue, attention to detail, and delight in anecdotes that she admired in Boswell. For a woman who loved literature, a woman who reveled in words, using her forte to write down her life — even painful parts — must have provided Inge with pleasure. I believe it's likely she found a certain comfort and confidence in securing the details of significant personal events, in holding on to meaningful emotions and thoughts, in re-reading her own poignant writing, and in creating the potential for sharing it all — that is, letting others in the future know who she was and how she saw herself, where she fit in and where she didn't.

As for Professor Pottle, evidently Inge stayed in touch with him long after her life at Yale. In October, 1983, more than 30 years after earning her Ph.D., in a letter to her friend, Marja, Inge wrote: "My dissertation director, Frederick Pottle, wrote to me today, mentioning [his serious spine-related health issues] … [A]ny shock or injury to that region would be fatal, he knows. He is 86 but still works every day at the Boswell office at Yale. Seems to me his devotion to his work keeps him alive."

THE UNITED STATES OF AMERICA

No. 6275673

CERTIFICATE OF NATURALIZATION

DEPARTMENT OF JUSTICE

Petition No. 34623

Personal description of holder as of date of naturalization: Age 25 years; sex Female ; color White ; complexion Olive ; color of eyes Brown ; color of hair Black ; height 5 feet 7 inches; weight 105 pounds; visible distinctive marks None Marital status Single ; former nationality German

I certify that the description above given is true, and that the photograph affixed hereto is a likeness of me.

Inge Charlotte Probstein
(Complete and true signature of holder)

STATE OF CONNECTICUT
NEW HAVEN COUNTY } ss:

Be it known that at a term of the UNITED STATES DISTRICT Court of DISTRICT OF CONNECTICUT held pursuant to law at NEW HAVEN, CONNECTICUT on JULY 25, 1947 the Court having found that INGE CHARLOTTE PROBSTEIN then residing at 370 Temple Street, New Haven, Connecticut intends to reside permanently in the United States (when so required by the Naturalization Laws of the United States), had in all other respects complied with the applicable provisions of such naturalization laws, and was entitled to be admitted to citizenship, thereupon ordered that such person be and (s)he was admitted as a citizen of the United States of America.

In testimony whereof the seal of the court is hereunto affixed this 25th day of JULY in the year of our Lord, nineteen hundred and FORTY-SEVEN and of our Independence the one hundred and SEVENTY-SECOND

C. E. PICKETT
Clerk of the U. S. DISTRICT Court
By Dorothy V. Thurber Deputy Clerk.

It is a violation of the U.S. Code (and punishable as such) to copy, print, photograph, or otherwise illegally use this certificate.

*While Inge was a Yale graduate student,
she became a U.S. citizen.*

CHAPTER 15

JOB SEARCH,
TEACHING (BRIEFLY). THERAPY

In 1947, having earned her M.A. in English literature at Yale, Inge was
ready to teach. At the graduate school's placement office, she filled out
the appropriate forms to be a college instructor. One of the questions
requiring a response was "Religious affiliation or preference?" (Her notes,
in parentheses, explain that this question on employment applications
was soon dropped, thanks to the Fair Employment Practice Committee).
"If you are half-Jewish by birth, half-Christian by religious training,
what should you say?" she pondered in a later essay called "A Question
of Identity." Her answer: "None."

In that same essay, her notes say she got her first teaching position
because of a misunderstanding. "The college wanted someone on its
English faculty to represent the Jewish tradition"; her last name, Probstein, qualified her. "The fact that I knew so little of the Jewish tradition
proved something of a disappointment, and the following year, while
keeping me on, the school hired a better 'representative.'" Maybe Inge's
comment that she was hired because she was thought to be Jewish is
literally true, but it might be an example of her frequent self-deprecation,
especially since Inge herself considers the anecdote "amusing."

"I suppose many half-Jews with Jewish names have thought at times of changing their name to something more neutral," Inge wrote, "if not altogether Anglo-Saxon sounding. When I was little," she continued, "I used to find among my brother's school exercises papers signed 'John Touchstone'; as I later found out it is the English translation of his first name and of our family name. When I was in high school in this country I sometimes used as my middle name my mother's family name, Von Nordeck. But I never dared leave off my last name, of course." She did note that she understood some people's temptation "to pass," rather than risk the possibility of job discrimination or a quick judgmental reaction to a Jewish-sounding name. "[H]alf-Jew/half-Christian is just as much Christian as Jewish, only the Christian part doesn't seem to count. What most people want from others is simply to be treated as a person, a member of the human race; but it seems at times you have to be a white Christian to begin with."

One other religion-oriented situation irked Inge in the workplace. "I wish people in offices who have nothing better to amuse themselves would stop telling jokes about Jews when they think that none are around. Once in a while they may hit a half-Jew, and it hurts." Always open-minded however, she added, "What about jabs from the other side? We in America and in Western Europe live in a Christian culture ... [where] Jews are more frequently the receivers than the givers of such jabs. I don't know whether the punches travel in the reverse direction in predominantly Jewish culture. Perhaps so ..."

Inge became an instructor on the faculty of Douglass College (eventually New Jersey College for Women, ultimately part of Rutgers University). "Freshmen had a long reading list," she wrote. "It was a very good teaching experience." But while at Douglass, she suffered a serious depression that interrupted her career. She did not name a possible cause of the despondency, but from her treatment, one could assume her condition was connected to homosexual stress. At that strongly bigoted time in American society, homosexuality was mostly to be kept in the closet or risk blatant condemnation. Many considered it a pathological condition. One remedy for her depression was drastic: electroconvulsive therapy (ECT). Though radical, this was a popular psychiatric treatment in the 1950's, intended to relieve severe depression by producing electrically induced seizures in the brain of an anesthetized patient. It purposely associated homosexual desire with pain and unpleasant feelings. "The doctors felt I needed shock treatments, which scared me," Inge wrote. This kind of "conversion therapy" had neither scientific basis nor evidence that it worked but was known to be sought by homosexuals (or families of homosexuals) who wanted a "cure." It required multiple treatments and follow-up examinations per week, so hospitalizing the patient was necessary. (Ultimately this therapy was considered a "cure" for an illness that doesn't exist. But it was not until 1973 that the American Psychiatric Association declassified homosexuality as a mental disorder.) Though Inge wrote that Dr. Lo, her doctor, "was possessed by Freudian doctrine," she did not explain how that affected her treatment. Freud had written "Homosexuality is assuredly no advantage, but it is nothing to be ashamed of, no vice, no degradation, it cannot be classified as an illness." Perhaps because her doctor was a disciple of Freud, Inge found him consoling.

She had no medically knowledgeable friends or relatives to consult about this extreme procedure, so, though anxious about it, she followed her doctor's advice in submitting to it. One Yale colleague, Mary Dukeshire, visited her in the hospital and assured her, as Inge wrote, "it was to make me a servant to Jesus." Inge did not note her reaction to her friend's explanation, but just the fact that Inge remembered this classmate's comment many years later, when looking back on this harrowing time of her life, suggests its impact. My knowledge of Inge suggests to me that she remembered it because it was so outrageous — perhaps as questionable as the treatment itself may have been.

Writing about this distressing period in her life many years after the fact, Inge reflected on it with a bit of humor, touching on her political acuity: "I tolerated the treatments," she wrote, "especially as I was woken by the doctors to see the Kefauver hearings," the then current, highly popular televised Senate investigations of organized crime in interstate commerce, exposing corruption in public institutions.

What! This sentence stopped me. Did Inge really emerge from a rigorous ECT treatment to find humor in a political situation? Although her notes express her ever-present concern for government power and citizens' compliance or defiance — from her Third Reich childhood, through her Georgia racist college environment, through the rest of her life — in this recollection of her emergence from electrically induced brain seizures, I sense a bit of the autobiographer's creative — and satiric — license.

CHAPTER 16

CHARLOTTE. DIFFERENT DIRECTIONS

At the end of her hospitalization, Inge moved in with a friend from Douglass College, but her stay there was brief because "Charlotte seduced me, and I moved in with her." Charlotte remained an integral part of Inge's life. The two were partners for many years, and good friends even longer. The only complaint Inge expressed in her notes about their relationship was how hurt she was "when we went to Cape Anne, she [Charlotte] made a play for a girl accompanying us, despite her companion." In 1958, a few years after this upsetting incident with Charlotte, Inge wrote a poem called "Love's Philosophy." I do not know if some contemporary event initiated this poem, or if it reflected past sentiments, one of which could have been this hurtful Charlotte episode. Inge, inclined to bring literature to life, and life to literature, more often than not included literary figures in her own writing. Her poem "Love's Philosophy" is about lovers and traitors in known literary works. One stanza refers to "the sea that bared her bosom to the moon" (Wordsworth); another refers to "And this dark night in vain does Cresseid [Cressida] cry / On Troilus' name" (Shakespeare). This stanza is totally Inge:

> *I cannot add to love's philosophy*
> *Save this: when one's undone there's two*

To find another; and that loss of love
Is (unlike pain) its self-contained infinity,
Compounded to unloose a tie that's sure
To make it hurt, and hurt itself to gain
Another lover's perjured love, and slay him once again.

Hostility towards gays and lesbians in the 1950's world, possibly contributing to Inge's earlier mental breakdown and hospitalization, may have been a factor in Inge's decision to work in a less finger-pointing, non-academic environment. What is clear is that despite her desire for a career in sharing her passion for literature with students, she felt impelled to make a change and decided to look for another kind of work. She found it at the Girl Scouts of America National Headquarters, where she was hired as a filing clerk but was soon promoted to executive status. Inge's job was to investigate propaganda causing accusations that the Girl Scouts organization was Communist.

Not knowing Inge until more than 30 years later, I cannot imagine her in this 1950's role. From my decades later perspective, I can only picture this Girl Scout administrator as straight-faced and cynical, occasionally allowing a sardonic smile. In my mind, she would have considered the accusations absurd. But in the 1950's, Communism in this country was a charge some considered comparable to witchcraft in colonial Massachusetts.

The charge came about in 1953, when Florida radio personality Robert Le Fevre claimed the Girl Scouts' handbook promoted pro-world rather than pro-American allegiances. In 1954, the Illinois branch of the American Legion, following Le Fevre's lead, denounced the Girl Scouts for "subversive and un-American influences." An Illinois congressman presented to Congress a resolution to condemn the Girl Scouts, adding that the *Girl Scout Leader* magazine had recommended "certain pro-Communist authors." Evidently he was referring to Langston Hughes and his *First Book of Negroes*, which the magazine reviewed because of the book's "clear presentation of the history and accomplishments of the Negroe [sic] race …" Because Hughes had been called to testify in the McCarthy hearings, the Girl Scouts were additionally jeopardized just by association. (Inge's notes do not explain this background information. It is drawn from an online piece: "The Girl Scout Red Scare," August 7, 2014 by Ann Robertson.)

Inge's research placed her in the thick of the Girl Scouts' investigation. I imagine she enjoyed unraveling the storyline; I also imagine she was appalled by what she probably considered an absurd accusation.

After this investigating experience, Inge was ready for a total change. Charlotte must have been similarly inclined. In 1956, "Charlotte and I quit our jobs, hers for Applewhite Publishers and mine for the Girl Scouts to sail [on an Italian line] for Europe with about $2500 each."

It was 24 years since Inge had fled Germany with her mother. Her memories were vivid; her curiosity about modern Europe, especially Germany, compelling.

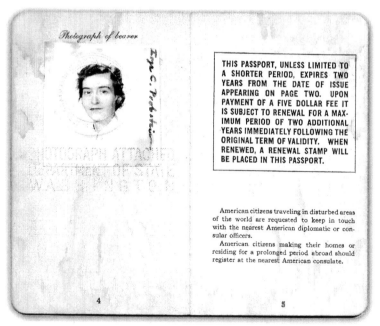

In 1965, 22 years after she escaped
from Germany, Inge returned.

CHAPTER 17

RETURN TO EUROPE

In England, their first stop, Charlotte developed boils on her buttocks, and was briefly hospitalized (city not noted), leaving Inge on her own for a while. She stayed at The York House, where on Sunday she spent some time "wandering at the beach in my thick coat and desert boots. The local girls with chaperones took delight in my get-together." The word "chaperones" is likely tongue-in-cheek; the reference to her inappropriate outfit is typically droll, self-deprecating Inge.

In Sicily, Inge and Charlotte asked two policemen the way to a recommended restaurant. "At the end of dinner, the two policemen arrived to pay for our dinner. One walked with Charlotte. The other put me on his motorbike. I was terrified to hang on; through the mountain he rode. Finally we were at the hotel and we had to tell that in America a girl does not entertain. They knocked on our door, and we were terrified."

From Taormina, at the toe of Italy, they traveled to Rome, where Charlotte again had need of a doctor. Inge recalled being directed to a hospital where "… the nuns drove white oxen in the fields" and "they had superlative food … Roman artichokes and wine, and they generously cared for Charlotte and me." While sight-seeing alone in Rome — the Appian Way, Keats' grave, St. Paul's, and the Spanish Steps — Inge came across a Frankfurt telephone book and decided to look for the name

Karl Rogge. Inge's notes may suggest this was a spontaneous decision, but I sense finding Karl, a.k.a. "Bubi," the dentist to whom her sister, Ruth, had been engaged, was in Inge's mind from Minute One of this planned this European trip.

Early in her notes, Inge had described Bubi as "a dear family friend until his family forced him into the SS." She was 12 when Ruth died; she was now 34. I cannot help but wonder about her feelings toward him now and what she anticipated in meeting with him.

Inge telephoned Karl; they arranged to meet when she got to Frankfurt. But first she and Charlotte, now recovered, travelled to Austria, where, in Salzburg, they stayed in a Gasthof with feather beds comfortable, luxurious and memorable enough to praise them on paper. She tried to arrange a side trip to her father's hometown, Quedlinburg, a town of half-timbered houses and cobblestone streets, north of the Harz Mountains, but that did not work out. So she and Charlotte continued on to Munich and to Ulm.

"Strange Fruit and Bitter Tea" (Inge's title)

In Herrlingen, a suburb of Ulm, where Inge had spent her early school years boarding at the Kinderheim, they stayed in the Rose Kreuz Inn. One can only imagine what mixed emotions Inge felt on returning to Germany: hearing and speaking her native language, recalling her love of school's academic challenges and then being banned from attending, remembering belonging to family and groups of friends and then being necessarily excluded, merging the memories of her family and happy childhood with the heartbreak of losing her sister and her father and her homeland. Amazingly, the innkeeper remembered Inge from her childhood days. "He asked me why I left Germany," she wrote. What was she to say? She wrote that she had not come back to Germany to talk about why she had left. "I did not want to remind him." She evaded the question. But the innkeeper was just the first to ask that same upsetting question: why had she left Germany? "It happened with all the Germans I saw."

Inge was especially intent on visiting the Kinderheim, where she and her brother, Hans, had been two of 18 young boarders in the late 1920's. Originally the school occupied a spacious, mid-19th-century mansion built by local metals industrialist Philipp Jakob Wieland. Even while Inge and Hans boarded there, the school was expanding into a private, non-denominational, coed school, officially registered as the Landschulheim Herrlingen. Eventually, 60 students boarded there. From the innkeeper at the Rose Kreuz Inn, Inge learned that the boarding school had been confiscated by the Nazis to train SS officers, and then converted back into a luxurious home for General Erwin Rommel, the "Desert Fox." But before that, in 1933, headmistress Anna Essinger, anticipating the Nazi onslaught, had gained permission from the parents of most of its Jewish boarders to transplant the school to England, re-establishing it as the Bunce Court School. Now, on this visit in 1956, Inge found her Kinderheim, the well-respected Landschulheim Herrlingen, "converted to an old people's nursing home."

Seated under an autographed portrait of Rommel in the Rose Kreuz Inn, the innkeeper droned on, complaining to Inge "how terrible the bombings had been, how little food there was during the last days of the war, how many had lost their lives, their relatives, their livelihood. I found myself pitying him," wrote Inge, "even while I was dimly conscious of the irony of our situation. He had asked me whether my father was still alive, and I told him that he had died in Germany in 1938. I don't believe it had occurred to this man that my father had died for reasons other than the greater glory of the German Reich."

In her long essay, "A Question of Identity," Inge reported on this return trip to Germany: "Most Germans I met seemed to welcome me as a returned prodigal, even though I usually mentioned in meeting strangers that I had emigrated in 1934. The year should have given them some clue to the reason for leaving. Very few brought up the 'Jewish business' and I certainly did not do so." Some people, she noted, remembered Hitler as "an uncultured man, an upstart who had led them to defeat."

At breakfast on Inge's and Charlotte's last day at the Rose Kreuz Inn, an American sergeant from Texas, hearing them speak English, thought he had found some American help. "What brings you to this Godforsaken dump?" the soldier asked. He wanted a favor of Inge and Charlotte: would they ask the innkeeper where he could fish for trout. He had heard there was good trout fishing in that area, and he wanted to spend the next week fishing, if he could find the right place. "I can't get this Kraut to drive me out there," the Texan grouched. "He doesn't even talk English." Inge understood the situation immediately: the innkeeper had no intention of helping the Texan. Clearly, she saw "[the innkeeper] wanted to punish the American soldier."

In Frankurt, Karl (she referred to Bubi by his given name in her notes here) and Inge met daily for a few mornings at cafés. Cafés were Karl's choice rather than his home because "his wife was jealous to hear any reminiscences of my sister, to whom she felt he was still emotionally attached ... He did talk quite a bit of Ruth ... It was obvious that he still loved her ... He brought photographs of her I had not seen, and he told me that in '33 he had transferred her ashes to a cemetery near him, where he could see to it that the grave was properly kept. This, he told me, got him in trouble with the SS, who denied him promotions in rank for several years."

I try to imagine Inge and Karl re-connecting in their native surroundings. He had been a key figure in her childhood and *the* key figure in her sister's life and tragic death. How could this meeting trigger anything but raw emotions? Yet, when I read what Inge wrote about those meetings, I realized she did not convey excessive feelings. Rather, her narrative is a rational account, tinged with her own calm insight. How typically Inge. In this writing about meeting Karl, I discern an example of Inge's core strength. Thirty-four years old, having spent much of her life steeling herself to handle extraordinary challenges, she was well-fortified to deal with this formidable event. Picturing Inge ready to meet Karl made me think back to her summary of her Yale paper on Lewis Carroll's *Alice in Wonderland* and *Through the Looking Glass*. From the White Knight episode, she had concluded "[O]ne ought, in any event, be prepared to see the world of sense upside-down … ."

Karl told Inge that during the war he was drafted into the Wehrmacht (Nazi armed forces) and had fought in Finland. He was married, but because his wife was in Frankfurt and he was held by the British as a prisoner of war after the Allied victory, they had to live separated for a period of years. One day after the war, when his wife was working as an interpreter for the American forces, she was hit by an American jeep. What seemed like minor injuries developed into total spine paralysis. "Dr. Rogge," wrote Inge, "was now the man of all work at home, doing the washing, the ironing, the cooking." But he still had a job, he assured Inge. He was administrator of dental care for the city's school children. He had never practiced as a dentist, he explained, as he "could not bear having to hurt people in the mouth." Above these last quoted words of Karl, Inge heavily inked a large prominent question mark. "Really?" I imagine her silently asking herself. I picture her listening to him — straight-faced, eyes widened incredulously. I imagine her inadvertently raised eyebrows as she wondered if the possibility of hurting a patient really troubled him. Or was she wondering if he was trying to impress her with his personal sensitivity, hoping to assure her he was still the kind, compassionate Bubi she knew, despite his having joined the Nazi Party and fighting for Nazi Germany?

On the morning of their last café meeting, Inge and Karl talked about Hitler and National Socialism: "Karl spoke calmly but with quiet conviction. Over coffee, he sought to convince me that if Hitler had won the war, Germany would have become a democracy with Hitler at the helm. Also, if Hitler had won, there would never again be persecution of the Jews (after he had eliminated them) [Inge's parentheses]. Hitler, he said, had made a terrible mistake in that respect … Hitler's anti-Semitism was a mistake that Hitler never intended." According to Karl Rogge, wrote Inge, "Hitler would have lived in peace with the world.

"What could I say? I couldn't believe it, and he needed to believe it … I was amazed at his ideas … I don't remember whether I argued or not. I hope I did not, for I realized later that he needed to cling to these ideas to justify his own past."

Reading and re-reading Inge's calm account of Karl's conversation, I came to sense that Inge did *not* argue. Judging from my 18 years as her student in lively, sometimes argumentative, literature class discussions, I remember her always listening respectfully to classmates' conflicting opinions and interpretations. Inge respected her students' opposing arguments, avoided judgement, and invariably maintained direct eye contact with the speaker. Her body language rarely revealed her mind.

"Apart from his opinions about Hitler," she wrote about Karl, he "was the same affable and gracious self he had always been to me and my family in the past. It was a strange series of coffee hours. What had happened to him in the intervening years was more than sad."

"More than sad" describes a letter Karl must have given to Inge at one of their café meetings, after having kept it for 22 years. (An image of the original letter in Ruth's handwriting follows this translation.)

Dear, dear Karl -

I am at the end! Life has been beautiful - but I don't want to fight any more.

You are the only man I have ever loved. I wish you all the best my darling. My last wish is that you don't go and see my parents, please. Because I know you don't like doing this. I also don't want any of your relatives to visit. Maybe just for the funeral.
Goodbye until we see each other again.

Your Ruth

Lieber lieber Paul –

ich mache Schluß. Das Leben
ist so schön, aber ich bin mir
zu schade dazu, unter die Räder
zu kommen.
Du bist der einzige Mann, den
ich geliebt habe (kitschiger Roman)
Ich wünsche dir alles alles Gute,
Liebling.
Meine letzte Bitte an dich
ist, nicht zu meinen Eltern
zu kommen – ich weiß wie
ungern du das tust. –
Auch von deinen Verwandten
soll niemand kommen.
Höchstens zur Beerdigung.
Auf wiedersehen, später
Deine Ruth

Handwritten letter from Ruth to Bubi (Karl).

After Karl, the one other person Inge wanted to see on her return visit to Frankfurt was Else Körner, one of her mother's former boarders in the Bauhaus-style community, whom Inge had loved to visit as a child. She remembered Fräulein Körner's room filled with plants and fine furniture. Else and Amelie had kept in touch during the war, intensifying their friendship through frequent correspondence, and Inge believed that her mother, now living in Lansdowne, a suburb of Philadelphia, considered Else her closest friend, though they were continents apart.

"My mother leaned on Else's good sense, her concern for the family, her perspectives, her humanity," Inge wrote. They had sent each other four- and five-page letters, always "in the stiff and steep 'Gothic' hand we had all learned in school but had forgotten as soon as possible." Now, in 1956, after many years on the waiting list, Fräulein Körner had a comfortable three-room government-sponsored apartment, and she was happy to cook a traditional German-style spring dinner for Inge: new potatoes, ham and asparagus. After Inge's café meetings with Karl, this visit was a welcome change. Here Inge felt calm, relaxed, "at home." Here she was not being asked why she had left Germany. Here she was not conversing with Nazi sympathizers or resentful Germans. And in the hospitality and congeniality of Fraulein Körner's apartment, she was not encountering the city's significant structural changes — both wrecked and reconstructed — of post-war Frankfurt. With Fräulein Körner, now in her 50's, Inge was enjoying the company of a respected old friend from her childhood. She was relishing the companionship of someone who had defied the Nazis.

A long-time executive secretary to the head of Frankfurt's largest city hospital, Else Körner had been fired when her boss asked her to join the Nazi party and she refused. Although she did find a job in another municipal agency, she struggled to survive. On Sundays during the war, she told Inge, she would ride her bike several miles to the country outside Frankfurt to visit her aging parents and see to their needs. The ride became simultaneously routine and dangerous, as she had to be alert to cars passing her on the rutted roads as well as to the whirr of low-flying planes, and she had to be ready to jump into a ditch along the road whenever bombs fell. Her one successful effort during the war, Else went on to explain to Inge, was as head volunteer air raid warden, a civilian job not requiring Nazi membership. "Else was supervising 20 women volunteers in the Römer [Frankfurt's medieval city hall] ... when the Old City of Frankfurt was fire-bombed ..." Surrounded by burning buildings, "Else told them their only escape was the River Main; they were to swim downriver and meet her on the dry land at the railroad station as soon as they could. All the women were saved," Inge wrote, adding that she noticed Else's slight smile as she ended her story, indicating to Inge a sign of modest pride in her significant accomplishment. Before leaving Frankfurt, Inge accompanied Else to visit Else's aged mother, "now living with Else's sister and her husband, a Lutheran minister who had defied the Nazi regime all along, but like Else, in a private and stoic manner."

When Inge was ready to leave Germany, Else wanted to accompany her to the railroad station. "We stopped for a coffee in a little bar," Inge noted, "and talked with two young Americans in Army uniforms. They had been stationed in Frankfurt for several years and were talkative and friendly. When we asked them if they had learned any German, they grew disdainful. 'What,' they demurred, 'what indeed is there to talk about with these Krauts?' If Else had heard this, she gave no indication of it whatsoever, although her English was perfect."

Inge does not mention Charlotte in her travels in Frankfurt; her notes are in the first person singular. But when she wrote of leaving Germany, she did refer to "we." Perhaps Charlotte was with her there, but because Inge's meetings with Karl and with Else Körner were deeply personal sequels to her childhood in Germany, she may have wanted to experience them alone. If Charlotte was in Frankfurt with her, Inge's memoirs about Karl Rogge and Else Körner suggest that what mattered most to her about this part of their trip were her own two meaningful, poignant reunions.

CHAPTER 18

WALKING WITH WORDSWORTH

From Germany, Inge and Charlotte traveled to Paris, then to London, from which they made several side trips. The first was to Leamington, 81 miles north of London, famous for its natural springs, "where we enjoyed a bath in the municipal 'Anstalt" [establishment]," wrote Inge. Another was to "Wordsworth Country," where they reveled in their walks in the Lake District in Cumbria, England's most northwest county. Inge's Ph.D. in English literature had given her profound knowledge of Wordsworth's work; among her papers is a ten-page essay on possible influences on his poems, i.e., Milton, the Stoics, Christianity. She must have exulted in the opportunity to personally see the natural environment that had inspired the English Romantic poet she revered. I imagine her wandering about these hills, valleys, and lake areas, imagining Wordsworth doing the same. She knew he had defined poetry as "the spontaneous overflow of powerful feelings: it takes its origin from emotion recollected in tranquility." Perhaps tranquility describes this last part of Inge's European trip — this peaceful immersion in the beauty of nature, a rewarding salve after her visit to Germany.

While Inge enjoyed the tranquility, I sense more intense contemplations must have ignited her mind. For Inge knew very well how Wordsworth deeply lamented the loss of the innate "poetic spirit" of innocent childhood. In his *Ode on Intimations of Immortality*, the poet claims once a person matures, the reality of mortality overrules his childhood innocence, and only an active imagination lets him get past the natural despair of aging. If Inge had her Wordsworth studies in mind, she understood the poet's claim that the grief which inevitably accompanies maturity forever clouds a person's undiluted joy in nature. As an adult, Wordsworth alleged, a person must then willfully try to make nature create cheerful moods, as it is the person, not nature, which has changed. I wonder if Inge had to conscientiously, willfully, create a mood of cheerfulness in her Lake Country strolls. Perhaps she, more than the average traveler there, genuinely understood and experienced the depth of Wordsworth's *Ode on Intimations of Immortality*.

Wordsworth held a secure place in Inge's extensive mental literary storehouse. Years later, when prefacing her autobiography, just before she began describing her joyful childhood world: "hiking in the nearby mountains with my family, ... coming home to a fine winter supper with freshly baked rolls and cheese," — she quoted the opening of Wordsworth's Ode:

> "There was a time
> Where meadow, grove, and stream
> Did seem appareled in celestial light."

If Inge felt in sync with Wordsworth as she and Charlotte strolled through the Lake District, I sense she was reflecting on the poet's need to reclaim, to salvage, to willfully create a genuine joy in nature. A serious Wordsworth scholar, Inge may have realized that his perspective pre-echoed her own vantage point. And the immutable memories of heartbreak that halted Inge's happy childhood may have affirmed to her Wordsworth's mid-Ode question about his own naïve, euphoric childhood relationship with nature:

> "Where is it now, the glory and the dream?"

89

If Inge felt in sync with Wordsworth in her wanderings through the Lake District, I hope she was feeling a more intellectual, profound agreement with the Ode's conclusion:

> "Thanks to the human heart by which we live
> Thanks to its tenderness, its joys and fears
> To me the meanest flower that blows can give
> Thoughts that too often lie too deep for tears."

Or perhaps the words of Wordsworth's *Tintern Abbey* more accurately reflected Inge's thoughts on that visit:

> "For I have learned
> To look on nature, not as in the hour
> Of thoughtless youth; but hearing oftentimes
> The still, sad music of humanity"

From England's Lake District, Inge and Charlotte went on to Carlisle and finally Liverpool, where they boarded a Canadian line back to the United States.

CHAPTER 19

NYU MISFORTUNE. "NORMALIZATION"

Inge looked forward to making a new start in the life she really wanted — teaching the literature she loved. She began her search for a college level position, but evidently she was not successful. In August, 1958, she signed a contract with New York University's Reading Clinic, in which Dr. Smith, an administrator, promised Inge her students would not be below a tenth-grade reading level, and they'd be either seniors in high school or college freshmen.

"I liked the idea of teaching at NYU," she wrote, "and being near a university library once more." Early in September she rented an apartment and had a complete medical check-up. Having suffered bouts of hepatitis twice (her notes do not mention when), she wanted to be sure she was in good health. On September 8, 1958, she wrote in a journal: "Felt fine physically (except tired from moving, I thought) and fine mentally. Had confidence in myself, liked my job and associates from the start. Felt good to be making a decent salary. (Had about $20.00 to live on until October 1; rent paid for September, of course, in advance.)"

On September 10, she was assigned to fifth-grade readers, boys 11 to 15. They were "terrific discipline problems at first but I thought I would try," she remembered, assuming that according to her contract she "could be transferred to another class if things did not work out." But she surprised herself: she enjoyed the challenge. "Loved the teaching and the class despite the problems," she wrote. Her teaching hours were long, followed by required attendance at frequent afternoon faculty meetings. And on the urging of the director, she enrolled in three graduate courses scheduled for evenings and Saturdays. Understandably, with her overloaded timetable she began to feel overtired and rushed; not understandably, she began to have frequent bouts of nausea. Her doctor advised taking two days off to have some lab tests, but the Reading Clinic's assistant director would not grant permission. "He seemed upset that I might be ill," she noted, indicating he was more concerned about her not being in her classroom than about her health.

Except for missing one faculty meeting because of nausea, Inge persisted in keeping up with her schedule. To add to her concerns, NYU's payroll department claimed some problems, and she and seven other new faculty instructors did not receive their salaries. Now financially strapped, Inge tried to get a $60.00 loan from a local bank — she was accustomed to living on a bare minimum — but because she had a new job and a new residence, the bank denied her request.

On October 8, she had to call in sick. She had Asian flu, a global pandemic raging since 1957. Even so, in two days, despite occasional fever, nausea and fatigue, Inge went back to school, having decided she'd keep teaching and just leave the classroom for a few minutes if the nausea overwhelmed her. A week later, on October 15, NYU sent her a letter requesting her resignation "for reasons of ill health."

"I was dumbfounded," she wrote, for by this time she was feeling better. Refusing to resign, she sought aid from Legal Counsel, which advised her to "sit it out and see." While absorbing the shock of her situation and awaiting further instructions from Legal Aid or the American Association of University Professors (AAUP), which never came, she worked in the university library on Renaissance literary research. Literature was her safe haven; in the study of literature, she found some comfort.

Academic, administrative, financial, and personal health problems mounted, reinforcing each other and resulting in extreme stress. Inge consulted with a school psychiatrist at NYU, wondering if she should go to a hospital for a two-day rest. He told her that "a hospital was no place to face one's problems," and that she "probably needed psychiatric help and could have psychosis over this whole mess." On October 31, she received written notice that she was dismissed as of October 15, "for inability to carry out my responsibilities." Inge appealed to the State Labor Board, which advised her she must file in a civil court. Attempts to seek help from other legal and university-associated organizations proved just as useless. Advised by her lawyer and friend, Anne Dix, to give NYU written notice of her legal complaint, she hand-delivered letters to Dr. Smith, with whom she had signed the contract to teach in the Reading Clinic, and to NYU Dean McGhee.

NYU paid her through the end of October, but not before the combined anxieties overwhelmed her. Totally discouraged, she left New York for a weekend in New England. (She did not write whom she visited or with whom she went.). But when she returned two days later, she was distraught enough for Anne Dix and a Dr. Reuben Greenspan to admit her to Bellevue Hospital, a public hospital specializing in helping patients with mental problems. Five days later she was discharged in her own custody, but feeling exhausted from her Bellevue experience and "not ready to face NY problems." She left three days later for Atlanta, looking forward to a week of "rest and regeneration." First she arranged with a Dr. Blumenthal, a psychiatrist, for further help when she returned. "I had an excellent week at my college," she wrote. "Worked, played, attended lectures, felt well enough to settle my affairs and get to work."

Considering her upbeat mood on her return to New York, I was surprised to see that her detailed recounting of this whole NYU experience notes that Dr. Blumenthal and Anne Dix re-admitted her to Bellevue. No further explanation. Bellevue was overcrowded, she wrote — "we slept in the hall" — so she was moved for brief stays to other psychiatric hospitals. About one move she wrote that she was "committed by [a] judge," even though she had offered to "go as [a] voluntary patient ..." Again, no further explanations.

In retrospect, she tallied the results of her NYU experience:

1. *Lost my apartment (eviction notice)*
2. *Blue Cross policy lapsed*
3. *Unpaid phone bill*
4. *Mother upset & worried needlessly*
5. *Lost 5 pounds from strain*
6. *Tooth infection [had to remain in Bellevue unattended]*
7. *Strain and worry*

Depression overwhelmed Inge several times, causing brief breakdowns and short stays in rehabilitation centers. In a letter to her mother during one of these times, Inge wrote objectively of her situation, accepting it as necessary. She sounded upbeat about feeling better, and told her mother not to worry as she looked forward to leaving rehab soon.

Knowing Inge from the mid-1980's to her death in 2006, I was stunned to read about these mental breakdowns. The humor, intelligence, and warmth she projected in our adult-education literature class belied such serious problems in her past. In addition to enjoying Inge's love of literature and her wit, we students did learn from informal class conversations a little more about her: she was a gourmet cook, a classical music afficionado (especially chamber music), a painting dilettante, and a follower of current politics (leaning liberal). But we never knew her personal story, her traumatic childhood in Germany, and the subsequent challenges she faced early in her career, including serious bouts of depression.

At this time of her NYU hiring/firing/health problem, she was living in Greenwich Village. The 1969 Stonewall riots were years ahead, but the Village was widely known to be a relatively comfortable home to many gay and lesbian residents. In the 1950's, a large part of society patently demeaned gays and lesbians, considering them odd, sinful, criminal, diseased, or at least sick. And if society repeatedly labeled a person "deviant," both blatantly and subtly disparaging her, no matter if that gay person lived comfortably, naturally, she was inevitably aware of the way society categorized her. Even just subconsciously, every time a gay person looked in a mirror, she may have unavoidably seen that same society-condemned, peculiar person. In the 1950's, a homosexual woman lived in an insecure, vulnerable reality, possibly causing self-doubt, instability, and depression. Psychiatrists confirm that the pressure of being homosexual in the 1950's understandably could cause overwhelming anxiety, intensified by outright social and political condemnation and accusations. An "incorrect" sexual orientation could keep a person from being hired or cause a person to be fired. Did Inge's sexual orientation affect her attempts to secure a good college-level teaching position, negatively influencing academic administrators? Academically, she was more than qualified.

Did Inge want to be "cured"? She had already undergone severe treatment, ECT, earlier in that decade. Notes written late in her life (judging from the scratchy handwriting) mention "the process of so-called 'normalization'" when she lived in the Village. I believe it is significant — or at least curious — that she did not write about this procedure in earlier accounts of this chronological time of her life.

The word "normalization" has opposing meanings, but Inge's intent seems clear. Present-day articles on this subject define "normalization" as learning to accept as "normal" behavior that was earlier considered "abnormal." But from what follows in Inge's notes, I assume she meant learning to change one's sexual behavior from what society considered "abnormal" to what society then accepted as "normal." Accounts of such attempted procedures for that second purpose of normalization exist but are mainly directed only to "abnormal" (homosexual) boys. In 1920 Freud had written (*The Psychogenesis of a Case of Homosexuality in a Woman*) that "in general to convert a fully developed homosexual into a heterosexual does not offer much more prospect of success than the reverse." Success would mean making heterosexual feelings possible, not just eliminating homosexual feelings.

"Normalization" didn't work for Inge. According to her notes: "My first 'victim' was an author of many novels, back from Spain. He bought me books, and made me feel that I, having been a lesbian, in no way ruled you out. My second was my teacher at the New School. [That was where she was taking NYU-required evening courses.] He could not wait for dinner, but assaulted you at once … Then there were assorted men, teaching at NYU, where I had a job in the Reading Institute, … then an engineer that worked with Oppenheimer. All this was too much for me," she wrote, and "I winged it to Atlanta" for a week.

In this same late-in-life scrawl, Inge summarized her hospitalization stays through the years. The writing is barely legible, and the dates are not noted, but included twice at Philadelphia Psychiatric, where she was grateful for "a great chance for painting," and twice at Haverford State Hospital. "In my last hospitalization [not stated where] … a psychiatric worker named Helen put me on lithium," a mood stabilizer for alleviating severe depression. Inge added that she was on it for years. A curious few lines about staying at psychiatric rehabs close that worn, scratchy-handwritten page of loose-leaf, lined paper: "My secret, in every case I failed the doctors. In my last hospitalization I was helped by Helen," whom Inge called a "psychiatric worker." This seems to be a jibe at her psychiatrist, while emphasizing help by a staff subordinate. [Note: To administer lithium, Helen had to have been a psychiatrist or a nurse following a psychiatrist's orders.] But if Inge's "secret" — that is, "I failed the doctors" — suggests some patient-psychiatrist antagonism, these lines, part of a rough copy of a longer piece [not dated] might confirm it:

> "What's this hostility, you ask,
> Tell me the meaning of it.
> Didn't I give you answer?
> At least two or three.
> Or did you give the last
> To me? I knew I couldn't

Settle it with jargon, not with you,
So "transference," "projection" which
I tried, did not provide protection.
At that I think you took
Your stethoscope or else
Read off some gauge; and since
I knew you read me, tried again
To put a bold face on and
To be honest. This was true.
And what I said was so.
I told you it was simple;
Wanting a human being to be so;*
But you were so damned competent
That when I was upset
I couldn't tell you no.
Why did that make you angry? You?
Or did you sense I'd won that round,
And so, of course, hit back
At me, the patient. Ow!
I'd never ask you to explain,
For I respect your office
And your individuality, as you do me.

*my bold italics

    I cannot claim to know the circumstances that initiated those confrontational words to her psychiatrist. Nor can I know Inge's mental state when she wrote them. But her exasperation — her fury, her intimidation — seems clear. In my reading, the key is in the lines I made bold: *I told you it was simple; Wanting a human being to be so.* That's all she wanted: to be respected as a human being, not to be categorized or judged as a homosexual, a Jew (or half/Jew), or any other "species" — just a human being.

CHAPTER 20

TEMPLE UNIVERSITY

In the 1960-61 school year, Temple University in Philadelphia hired Inge as an instructor in the English Department. The following year she was named an assistant professor.

"Even though it was like a factory, the students were very good," she wrote in her brief notes about Temple. "Freshmen had *Portrait of the Artist as a Young Man,* and many good works. They were very receptive. Had one student who would be a mechanic, but said he would never forget *Portrait.* [Also] I taught a graduate seminar in how to do research. That was very good. [And] we played with the text of Boswell's *Journal.*"

Among Inge's papers is a typed carbon copy of a facetious poem she wrote, probably about this time (it mentions Mitten Hall, Temple University's community center), regarding students who do not take their assignments seriously. It is a parody on the 17th-century poet Andrew Marvell's "To His Coy Mistress," in which one theme is mortality — that is, how little time we have on earth and therefore cannot keep procrastinating. Like Marvell's poem, Inge's full lampoon is a three-stanza monologue in rhyming couplets. Here are just a few lines from Inge's "To His Coy Freshman":

Had we but world enough and time,
Your theme, Miss Wunder, were no crime;
We could sit down in Mitten Hall,
Have coffee and discuss it all:
Thou by the coke machine mighs't find
A pickled dill; I o'er the kind
Of coffee should complain — I should
Have had a drink before the Flood

...

An hundred hours should go to praise
Thy modifiers, though misplaced,
Two hundred to adore each comma,
And thirty thousand to your grammar;
An age at least to every shred
Of sense that you have in your head.
For, lady, you deserve this C
Nor would I change your grade to E.

I picture Inge grinning as she applied this 17th-century classic poem to a 1960's freshman. I have no idea with whom she shared this, or *if* she shared it.

But she did share a much more sophisticated poem with members of the CEA, the College English Association. The 1966 issue of the CEA CRITIC published a poem Inge wrote specifically for this professional organization of college English teachers. Her poem assumes most of those readers were steeped in Henry James' literature and alert to arguments current college English teachers were having about James' symbolism. CEA scholar-members would appreciate Inge's intelligence and humor in her satire — or perhaps, mockery of — the various interpretations of James' symbols. In typical Inge fashion, she seasoned her own extensive literary knowledge and understanding of the Henry James controversy with her own down-to-earth sense of humor. Even her subtitle spoofs the subject: "Jacobite" refers to advocates (maybe worshippers) of King James II. *What Maisie Knew* is Henry James' novel about a child of divorced parents, the parents' new spouses, and two governesses. For some explanations of references in the poem's lines, I've added some literary clues. (See page 102.*)

What Maisie Knew:
A Note on the Jacobite Controversy

> *The Beast in the Jungle,*
> *The Turn of the Screw,*
> *Are Freudian to many,*
> *Miltonic to few.*
>
> *The Wings of the Dove*
> *Are the Spoils to the Point,*
> *The Maltese a Falcon;*
> *The crux is the joint.*
>
> *The Pupil's a liar*
> *And James a voyeur,*
> *A masochist-sadist*
> *Boston malheur.*
>
> *James' centers of vision,*
> *No voice will deny,*
> *Look dim in the trousers*
> *But sharp in the eye.*
>
> *In Marcher and May, (1)*
> *In Quint and in Bly, (2)*
> *James shows he is terribly*
> *Terribly sly.*

The sphinx is a lily,
The lily a bell
The bell tolls rachitic;
It's puzzling as hell.

The garden as symbol
By Troy is proposed;
The symbol as garden
By Tate is opposed.

If Warren was right
Then Edel may have said (3)
What Geismar distorts
With that fig in his head. (4)

If Anderson tells us (5)
What Holland denies, (6)
The Swedenborg myth was (7)
The beam in his eyes.

If his failure is Marxist,
To some this means Sex,
The exile at Lamb House(8)
His Fountain Perplex. (9)

The Mote in the Carpet,
The American Scene
Is only his figure
For all that's obscene.

Inge Probstein,
Temple University

*Some literary clues to Inge's poem satirizing Henry James' works and his critics:

1. Characters in James' *The Beast in the Jungle*.
2. Quint = first ghost (valet) in *Turn of the Screw* Bly Manor = setting of *Turn of the Screw*
3. Leon Edel, 20th c. authority on Henry James
4. Refers to *The Fig Eater* by Jody Shields, story re murder of "Dora," based on Freud's patient
5. Quentin Anderson, historian claimed Henry James influenced by his father's religion (Swedenborg)
6. Laurence B. Holland, historian claimed Henry James *NOT* influenced by his father's religion
7. Henry James, Sr., theologian, follower of Swedenborg's teaching
8. Lamb House = Henry James' house in London
9. *The Sacred Fount*, by Henry James

CHAPTER 21

LIFE IS GOOD

Nothing in Inge's notes explains why she left Temple University in 1966 and began teaching in 1967 at Cheney, a state college outside Philadelphia. Would she earn a higher salary (always welcomed, as she was supporting herself, her mother, and her brother)? Would she be granted higher status? Did she prefer a small, suburban campus to a large city school? Would she rather drive about 18 miles to Cheney's spacious campus instead of about 25 miles in traffic to Temple's crowded urban location? I found no answers in her notes. Nor did I find any evidence of dissatisfaction or teaching problems at Temple. In fact, post-mortem evidence suggested her relationship to Temple had been a positive one. In 2008, two years after Inge died, the minutes of the meeting of Temple University's Budget and Finance Committee and Executive Committee of the Board of Trustees mention the establishment of "a quasi-endowment ... from the estate of Inge Probstein, for the purpose of creating the Inge Probstein Endowment for English."

Whatever her reason for leaving Temple remains a mystery to me. But from her notes about her life at this time — home, friends, career — she seemed mostly satisfied. She shared a house in Lansdowne, a

Philadelphia neighborhood, with her mother, Amelie. Having been through so much trauma together — Nazi Germany, immigration in America, Inge's mental health problems — they now had the pleasure of enjoying each other's company, and Inge specifically noted that they got along very well. Amelie did the cooking; Inge paid the bills. Hans spent weekends with them, which Inge strongly resented. Hans had never really recovered from his last-minute, lucky escape from Nazi Germany, and he'd never adjusted to his immigrant status in America. He always sensed others considered him "second class." Nor had he ever become financially self-reliant, depending instead on Inge's help. Though Inge and Hans had lived comfortably together in the strained conditions of their little Radnor house, when Inge was in high school and Amelie was a cook living nearby on the Dorrance estate, at this middle-aged point in their lives — Inge was 45, Hans, 51— Inge considered Hans unreasonably demanding. Around this time she wrote some notes entitled "My Brother." The first line is "Am I My Brother's Keeper?" Except for Hans' weekend visits, Inge's life at home was routinely gratifying.

And the family had a cat. Once Inge was an adult living in her own home, she was always devoted to a cat. She so enjoyed a rapport with her independent feline that she often mentioned its antics in letters to friends. One page in her autobiography notes suggests she started to write a poem about cats, but jotted down just a few words, and then crossed some out. I don't know if she ever finished the poem. From the scribbled notes, I gleaned the following:

> *Of the many kinds of love that exist*
> *There is first of all love for one's cat,*
> *Utterly solidly tender, stroking [unintelligible word] her silken face,*
> *Stroking the down beneath her chin*
> *This sort of love is replied by the cat*
> *In asking for even more.*

Several letters Inge mailed to me through the years were written on notecards flaunting a glossy cat on the front. And among her collected papers was a page torn from *Applause* Magazine, December, 1986, entitled "Cats." Besides quoting T. S. Eliot's poem, "The Naming of Cats," this page humorously notes "a list of famous cat lovers and cat haters." Among the former are Anne Frank, Victor Hugo, Edgar Allan Poe, Mark Twain, Lewis Carroll, and George Bernard Shaw. Among the latter: Adolph Hitler, Napoleon, and Henry III of France — Inge's humor clearly reflected.

Jottings in her daily journals suggest she did not lack friends. Old college classmates Ginny and Wendy kept in touch via long-distance phone calls and occasional visits. Inge kept a page cut from the *New Yorker*, an article by art critic Peter Schjeldahl on the Barnes Foundation, the world-renowned suburban Philadelphia art institution in the headlines at that time because of its plan to break its founder's will and move into the city. Across the top of the first page is handwritten (by Ginny, I think): "Hello, Inge. I remember well the happy day I spent with you at the Barnes!"

And in a letter to her good friend and former partner, Charlotte, Inge wrote of enjoying a day trip with a friend to Pennsylvania Dutch Country in Lancaster, Pennsylvania, where they admired Amish quilts, bought fresh produce in a farmer's market, and were especially captivated by the horse-drawn buggies and the Amish — "men wearing dark blue suits — no buttons — straw hats, beards, and the women in dark blue dresses, wearing black bonnets, ... contrasting curiously with a certain amount of blatant commercialization." She then suggested the irony of these Amish catering to well-dressed "Yuppies" and tourists like themselves.

As for Christmas cards to friends, Inge delighted in writing her own, always with her own personality and humor inherent in the lines, as in her 1982 greeting to some friends:

My dearest denizens of northern clime,
Having no Christmas card to send in time,
I take th'unfeathered nib, the ball point pen
To send my Christmas greetings once again.
I hope the snow continues to abate;
Let lumb'ring plow and ice-packed shovel wait
Until you can depart for sun-drenched Spain,
Where may your knees, dear Ruth, withouten pain
Bear you with blithe steps o'er the plain.
Pray you, dear Irwin, drive the rented steed
From Avis o'er the gently rolling mead
Shunning the windmills none of us would fight
If only we discerned: the roadmap's right.
The news from here is short. Semesters end
With students' outraged howls, but saints defend
Th'embattled teachers, ever patient drones
To murdered grammar and its living clones.
Charles' Christmas party was a great success.
To feed on ham, pate, and watercress
The goodly spirits came from far and near
To outwit still another startling year
Of Ronald Reagan's baleful governaunce —
I fear we've hardly got much chaunce —
But nonetheless I wish you for the naunce
Good chere, good yere, in all this daunce.

I can imagine Inge's self-satisfied smile as she included at least one reference to literature (battling windmills) and parodied Olde English words and spelling. The "Charles" who gave the Christmas party (line 18) was a Temple University English professor, Inge's very good friend and colleague whom she mentioned occasionally in our adult education class, and with whom Inge shared her love of literature and of teaching. Here is a rough copy of a letter to Charles after his Christmas party, noted in the above poem:

Dear Charles:

Though absence seemed my flame to qualify
I must say that last night it burned quite high.
What? Lit by Scotch, pate, and watercress alone?
Dear Charles, do not suspect 'twas so! Atone
For that suspicion when I tell you true:
Although the best of hosts is surely you,
Though you give parties with divine aplomb,
Though timid virgins leave their padlocked home
For such Lucullan feasts as you provide
To wits and beaux and beldames far and wide,
Though you are mired among the salad greens,
Betimes the used-up platters and terrines:
Always you are the centerpiece of my affection
And that, dear Charles, is a mature reflection.
It's you I love among the chattering din
Above the ebullient vaporescence of your gin.

Clearly, Inge loved a good party among good friends, and she loved to celebrate in witty words. I picture her as upbeat, delightful company in her own social settings. She liked good food, she liked to drink, she liked to socialize. And I imagine her friends loved her poetic way of communicating.

One more light-hearted poem from Inge to friends who were "car-less":

Let a Smile Be Your Safety-Net

Elisabeth and Peg, I must express my grief
On hearing that you're still without relief,
Without the Pontiac parts, without that mobile ass
(Though a prodigious eater-up of high-priced gas)
To bear your bundles and to fetch your store
From Acme or from Thriftway to your door.
You must be getting lean like Don Quixote
On your abbreviated table d'hote.
And how about the other trips you took
To get your hair cut or to buy a book,
To feed the one-armed bandit in Atlantic City,
To whirl in discos, plunder malls? A pity
That all these joys have been for weeks suspended,
That GM has thus dastardly extended
Your house arrest! But you have passed a test:
They also serve this sad economy who wait
For US parts that show up three months late.
You might have bought a Japan flivver or an Ayrab horse,
Instead you chose so wisely just to stay the course.

In serious or trivial matters, Inge's brainwaves liked functioning in words that worked in rhyme and rhythm and literary references. Even in the above poem, "Let a Smile Be Your Safety Net," written just to let friends know she was thinking about them, at least two literary connections appear (*Don Quixote;* Milton, *Sonnet 19:* "They also serve ... who wait ...")

As Inge's longtime student, I was aware of the depth of her literary knowledge, but not until I came to really know Inge — from her autobiographical notes — did I understand just how vividly integrated into her everyday life were characters of classical literature. She might refer to them humorously, but she knew well their essence and their relevancy to her message of the moment.

One long letter, which uncharacteristically contains no reference to a literary character, is Inge's draft to her friend Marja. Filling four 8½ x 11 pages, Inge extended her sympathy for this older friend's osteo-arthritis pain, then expounded on her own recent events and thoughts, i.e., attending a wonderful Monteverdi concert, after which she discussed the music with one of the violinists; the large class sizes assigned to her; and her struggle in the French language class she was taking. She explained that she'd wanted to ask her French teacher a very complicated question — in French, of course — about the text the class was studying: differences in Celtic and Indian representations of gods compared with Greek representations of gods. (*Everything interested Inge!* She was always ready to ask more questions, to seek clearer understanding — for her own knowledge as well as for discussion in our adult-education classes.)

"I had to phrase all of this in French and nearly expired finding the words," Inge admitted to Marja. Then Inge explained, likely in a heavy French accent, "my instructor interposed, 'Courage, Mademoiselle. Courage.'"

In my mind's eye, I can see "Mademoiselle" stammering to come up with the correct vocabulary but smiling and fully intent on succeeding. "Courage, Mademoiselle." Courage, I believe, is a quality Inge never lacked, especially facing an academic challenge. Courage plus determination. "Tomorrow we meet again," she continued to Marja, "and I must study my text of the lectures. I give three evenings a week to French because nothing can be accomplished without some study ahead of time."

But what I found most thought-provoking in this letter was Inge's candid explanation to Marja of her feelings toward their friendship. They had both spent a weekend at a nearby resort, and Inge was looking forward to returning to the lakeside inn.

"I will miss your presence at the table and going over to the lake," she wrote. "We really had a good time together. I only supported your arm. You gave a lot more to my being. As Buber would say, you confirmed me because you accepted me as a person in weakness and in whatever strength. I accepted/confirmed you in exactly the same way, but then I think your only weakness is physical. You don't walk so well. If what I'm saying is alien to you, read Buber. He feels that the essential contact between two human beings is acceptance, i.e., affirmation of the other's being. I always felt — and will feel — at ease with you because I felt you would overlook my immaturity and excrescences. At the same time, I felt I would "overlook" or accept your maturity, your superior insight and perspective because, so what, you have the advantage of a few years. In other words, I take you as philosophically as you take me. Isn't that a fair exchange?"

Coming across this reference to Martin Buber both delighted and frustrated me. Ever since I first became aware of this 20th-century, Austrian/Israeli philosopher's *I and Thou* (perhaps 50 years ago?), I have thought this book about relationships should be required reading. Although Buber may seem complex, his basic point examines the way towards positive relationships: accepting/respecting people as they are — that broad necessity of our human society (and what Inge sought in her poem to her psychiatrist — See Chapter 20).

Briefly, Buber explains two kinds of relationships: in one, a person fully respects and accepts, fully "*encounters*," another person or an object — that is, creates an *I-Thou* relationship. In the other, a person relates but keeps a sense of detachment as he "*experiences*" another person or object — that is, creates an *I-It* relationship. When I read that Inge, too, revered Buber, I felt a deeper link between us surging. Oh, how I wished I had shared Buber with her! At that same moment, a heartfelt sadness struck me as I regretted I'd never hear Inge discuss this idealist philosopher we both esteemed.

CHAPTER 22

THEN IT ISN'T

Teaching at Cheney initially gave Inge the challenge she wanted: to open young minds to the rewards of literature. She anticipated helping her students appreciate the power of words, of literature's capacity to bring insights, pleasure, and relevance to their own lives. And she was committed to helping them write clearly, to express themselves effectively.

Cheney was a small, rural Pennsylvania state college, the first historically Black college in the United States. (Two of Cheney's famous graduates were civil rights activist Bayard Rustin, 1937, and CBS news journalist Ed Bradley, 1964. Cheney College became Cheney University in 1983.) Inge wrote that to reach students who wanted to learn was enormously gratifying, also noting that she "easily made friends among the faculty," and enjoyed participating in school activities.

"At Cheney," she wrote, "I had a group who read Mann and Kafka. I met them in my office, and they were very good about understanding the work." No one was more energized than Inge about literature, and no one was more motivated to impart that zeal to her students. But as the years changed, so did circumstances at Cheney, and so did Inge. Eventually, for several reasons, no one was more frustrated.

Her discontent arose primarily from the size of the classes the school came to expect its faculty to teach. In one early 1980's situation,

Inge determined that the school administration had not prepared for the increased number of enrolled students. They assigned 60 or 70 to a class. After the first weeks of the semester, the administration promised that these outrageously large classes would be reduced to 30 or 35, but then rescinded their promise, and urged English students to take Social Science classes instead. When only five chose to leave Inge's class, administrators told her she must arbitrarily call out thirty names and order them to leave. Inge loathed being ordered to do this. Besides, this was in the fourth week of the semester. "Bad enough that these students should begin a new class in the fourth week of school. Three weeks of instruction have gone down the drain. These students will never again have the faith to enroll for a class that they need ...." Her irritation about the class size in another situation is clear in the notes she jotted in a letter to a friend: "School is in utter chaos ... enrolment of 474 students in 9 sections ... This averages out to 52+ per section; some of us have over 70, I *only* 46." (Cheney must have been going through some difficult times. Update: In 2021, Cheney reported a 13-1 student-teacher ratio.)

Inge never wanted to teach by lecturing; that was not her style. To be an effective teacher, she felt she needed to connect more personally with her students; standing in front of a large impersonal audience precluded that bond. How could she possibly get to know her students in such oversized classes? In my own experience in Inge's adult-education classes years later, Inge was both curious and caring about each student. Of course, our adult-education class was limited to 20 to 25, and most of us became "repeat students" semester after semester — a whole different story from Inge's college-teaching experience. She had wanted to encourage her college students to open and challenge their minds, to help them benefit from the rewards of literature and good writing. But under those teaching circumstances she was finding that harder and harder to do.

Her growing frustration was further exacerbated by the result of several concurring circumstances. Because classes were increasing in size,

Inge's enthusiasm for teaching was hampered. Cause and effect were in play, but Inge, growing older and perhaps more impatient, was tiring of the challenge she had so enthusiastically embraced, especially because she realized these negative circumstances would always be beyond her control. Cheney had open enrollment, so every high school graduate who applied was accepted.

Student apathy also played a role in her disenchantment. That was partially a result of class size, which clearly affected teacher response, which, going full circle, affected student initiative, or lack thereof. "The students are amiable," Inge wrote, "but 90% are utterly passive learners, [and] will not use their minds at all ... They just want you to *tell* them."

Inge was well aware that an effective teacher searches for connecting points to her students — that is, an intellectual basis or level ground from which teacher and student can comfortably move ahead together, discussing and examining individual insights. From my own 18 years of being a student in her class, I have a sense of her teaching technique. She would start class asking for the students' thoughts on specific issues or characters or the language of the assigned literature. I do not know the literature these students were assigned, but I cannot imagine Inge expecting a freshman to analyze irony in Beckett's *Waiting for Godot*. I believe she would never have assigned that perplexing play until she knew that her students understood reading required more than recognizing "what happens" in a story. Nor can I imagine Inge expecting her freshmen students to write an essay on the symbolism of rain in Toni Morrison's The *Song of Solomon* or Hemingway's *A Farewell to Arms*. From her notes I know Inge did not expect these young college students to be reading or writing at a high academic level; but she did expect their intellectual basis, the level ground of their reading experience, to include at least an understanding of why they were studying literature and why it was important to write clearly. She assumed college students were seeking an academic challenge, and she wanted them to come to understand that even if they didn't recognize it yet, dealing effectively in language, in appropriate words, would be increasingly valuable in their lives, not just in literature classes. And she wanted to help them recognize that studying literature and writing about literary issues would expand their minds and give them broader life-long benefits.

The seeds of her philosophy of teaching seem to have been sown in her early education in the Landschulheim Herrlingen, where encouraging independent critical thinking was the bottom line. That remained Inge's approach to education. That's what she wanted from her students; she needed them to be inquisitive, to want to seek meaningful insights, to discover the pleasure in interpreting. But first she needed them to charge up their brainpower.

I've tried to imagine Inge in these classes, perhaps assigning some basic classic books like George Orwell's *Animal Farm* or 1984. In my mind, I see her leading her students to discover symbolism and meaning, helping them illuminate the plot and the characters through discussion and writing. I imagine her assigning Lorraine Hansberry's *Raisin in the Sun*, or Nathaniel Hawthorne's *The Scarlet Letter*, and encouraging her students to think past the plot, to what the opening scenes or subtle descriptions revealed about the issues the characters faced. From my many years in Inge's literature classes, I think she would have wanted to impress on her students that there were no right or wrong answers, but they would have to filter the story through their own minds and consider serious responses to "what do you think?" According to her notes and my own experience as her student, she very much wanted to initiate classroom discussion, hear her students' insights. But circumstances at the school at this time seemed to hinder that.

In her notes, Inge wrote: "… when I taught my course in Romantic Poets [at Cheney] at the same level as I had taught it at Temple, a few vocal students complained that they could not follow, but the then department head, Dr. Oliver, defended my teaching by telling my students that they were being taught at a college level and weren't used to it. … [I]n 1967 and in the subsequent two or three years," Inge wrote, "we had a mix of students. The excellent students set a standard for the whole class and pulled the poorer students out of the morass of academic poverty." Then circumstances changed. "[I]n the name of democracy," Inge lamented, many colleges, including Cheney, began admitting students not necessarily qualified for college-level studies, at least not what Inge considered college-level studies. She compared the admission policy of the college to a basketball coach's guidelines. Would he allow "every person to qualify for the team regardless of the potential player's ability to play basketball?" Would he "take in basketball players who can't even dribble the ball?"

Equal rights for all? Yes, I think Inge would certainly agree. Equal opportunity for education for all? Yes, I think Inge would undoubtedly concur. Equal level of education for all? Not possible. Inge was teaching at — and expecting a response to — a level not comfortable to most of her students. And her students were accustomed to a level of teaching not comfortable to Inge.

Her disparaging notes continue: "While I disagree with the principle of 'democratic' admission to higher education, … I believe much could be done if the students admitted … had a strong motivation to succeed. But a lack of motivation, plus a 'lack of effort, attention, … [and] academic standards' produces a triple 'tragedy of waste': for the unqualified students' minds, the 'teachers' efforts, and the taxpayers' money." (According to Inge, over 90% of her students' educations were financed by grants and/or loans.)

Whether Inge expected too much of the students, or the students just didn't connect to Inge's method of teaching, more and more frequently she could not find that necessary common ground, that level of learning from which she could incite some curiosity and enthusiasm for literature. These students had succeeded in their pre-college education; they were high school graduates proud to be college students. But their prior education had not prepared them for the level of college learning Inge expected. Teacher and students were on different tracks, and she came to realize that she and they were just not the right match for each other.

Dr. Barbara Kardon, a faculty member in Cheney's Department of

Early Childhood Education at the same time Inge was teaching English there, did not find similar problems with her students' motivation. But her students, she explained, were mainly "mature women who were raising children and wanted to better their lives and the lives of their children. They had returned to school with a vengeance and were determined to succeed … They were very poor writers though," she admitted. Dr. Kardon's students were learning to succeed in a trade, a teaching career. Inge's students did not have the same incentive, and many did not understand what Inge wanted them to understand — that literature nourishes your knowledge of human conditions, that it broadens your thinking, that it expands awareness of the world, that it magnifies life, that it can bring awesome intellectual pleasure.

In the year Inge finally decided to retire, 1984, her discontent was burgeoning. "Oh, I knew how to get my students out of this lethargy," she wrote. "If I was willing to make a fool of myself, give some exaggerated pantomime of a character they were (supposedly) reading about, if I could produce some sort of slapstick comedy in class, they loved it. But one cannot clown one's way through agreement of subject and verb, through quadratic equations, or through the life cycle of the fern.

"Our students fail to distinguish between entertainment and learning. Their own intellectual development is absent as a motivation for learning. So long as the teacher is not 'entertaining' by the standards of say, The Cookie Monster or Michael Jackson, the majority of the class remains turned off; this is detrimental to the students and most dejecting to the teacher." Inge's frustration — and perhaps "burn-out" level— reached a peak and took her past her point of effective teaching.

Another dilemma existed by the time Inge decided to retire: she found increasing evidence of racism. Although this college was basically a Black institution — the administration and almost all the students were Black — Inge never felt uncomfortable until her last years of teaching. While early in her Cheney years, she had noted how she enjoyed the mixed-race faculty community working together, in her last years she wrote of how she regretted perceiving racial tensions.

I think Inge was neither naïve nor prejudiced; she clearly recognized and respected the cultural differences between herself and her students. In 1983, in a Cheney newspaper, she responded to an article about racism in Webster's Dictionary. The writer of the article, a Mr. Fred Wyche, had called the editors of Webster's "bigots" in their definitions of the word "brother." Inge wrote the following response:

FRIDAY, OCTOBER 14, 1983   THE REC

EDITORIALS ANI

LETTER TO THE EDITOR

Mr. Fred Wyche's article "Racism in Webster's" (The Cheyney Record, 9/30/83) springs from confusion and ignorance about dictionaries. Mr. Wyche cites two of Webster's definitions of the word BROTHER: 2. a fellow man and 4. a fellow black and then asks, "Will someone please explain to me the differences between 'fellow man' and 'fellow black' assuming that Webster's means fellow black man." He goes on to call the editors of Webster's "bigots publishing biased definitions."

Mr. Wyche, you missed the point. Of course "fellow man" as a definition for "brother" includes all men. You are confused in assuming that "fellow man" MEANS (your word) "fellow black man." Definition 2 is inclusive; definition 4 is exclusive.

The other day in my Speech class, I asked who had not given a particular speech. "The brother there," several students said. Not knowing his name (in a class of 64), I asked him, "Brother, will you speak next?" The class dissolved in laughter at my use (definition 2) of the word, since they use it and are used to it as meaning "a fellow black" (definition 4). I am white.

Dictionaries reflect usage; dictionary editors do not sit around making up definitions. Definition 4 reflects the fact that blacks use the word "brother" in this sense. When the word ceases to be used by blacks in this sense, definition 4 will drop out of Webster's. Think about it!

Inge Probstein
Professor of English

In her later years at Cheney, Inge was saddened that "relations between black and white faculty have become polarized … We who used to socialize easily now break up into color groups." Early in her years at

Cheney, she had not sensed racism, but she was becoming increasingly aware that "although black faculty members sometimes blast students for their lack of performance, no white faculty member dares do this, for this would be taken as racist by students." Finding this situation distressing, she noted she wished she could still enjoy the former cooperative effort of the bi-racial faculty, trusting they had all shared their one goal in common: educating these young students. Having been a victim of anti-Semitism, then a college student sensitive to Georgia racism all around her, and a homosexual woman living in a prejudiced culture that criminalized homosexuality, Inge was predisposed to deplore all intolerance. Years later, in our adult-education class discussions, I remember she was adamantly offended by prejudice of any kind.

While Inge was still on the Cheney faculty, she wrote a poetic toast to another English teacher, her friend who had already decided to retire. It reveals her humor, but also the degree of her discontent. After honoring this friend's dedication to trying to impart "the joys of reading, of clarity in writing, [and] thinking," Inge's typical poetic humor included references — as always — to classical literature. Her message was wickedly blunt:

> *I still maintain ours is a noble calling*
> *Although its nitty-gritty detail lately most appalling.*
> *The Augean stables of our students' prose*
> *We marginally swept five thousand times,*
> *But like the task of Sisyphus, there always rose*
> *Another pile of papers with the same old crimes,*
> *Endless assault and battery on English prose.*
> *Ours was Europa's fabled fate in full,*
> *Raped weekly by another bunch of bull.*
> *Best quit this scene of mayhem while you're ahead,*
> *Before the millionth sentence strike you dead."*

CHAPTER 23

HER POLITICS

Conversation in our adult education class often included issues currently in the news, so Inge's liberal views were evident, but as her student I knew nothing of the political causes she had defended or railed against in her earlier life or outside of class. Inge never talked about her past or her personal life. Not until she was gone, not until I had spent days and weeks and months exploring her papers and letters and newspaper clippings of published letters to editors, did I realize Inge's ongoing passion for every citizen's rights. Not until then did I learn of her determination to jot down her thoughts and to express them to friends, to newspapers, and to a Supreme Court justice. The deeper I delved into Inge's lifetime notes, the more "alive" she became to me, the more energized I felt in our relationship, the more I wished we could communicate.

Government and social policies at all levels — and their relationship to every citizen's rights — claimed a perpetual place in Inge's liberal-leaning mind. In retrospect, this thread of concern became undisputedly transparent. When only ten years old in Germany in 1932, she was aware of the distress Hitler's policies caused her family, and two years later, of their tragic personal consequences. An adolescent in America, she was saddened to see Depression victims having to beg for food in the great United States of America. A college student in blatantly racist Georgia, she was stunned that her classmates, as well as society all around her there, accepted demeaning non-white people as standard government policy. And I believe when, in her 20's she was hospitalized for depression intensified by public condemnation of homosexuality, she must have felt crushed by society's acceptable rejection of her. Wherever she was, government and social policy and their effect on individual citizens mattered to Inge.

I imagine Inge in a despondent mood concerning world news and what she called "super-state" power when she jotted down these lines. Several crossed-out words and filled-in changes indicate it's a rough draft of a poem. If she wrote more than what appears here (this ends with a comma and crossed-out illegible words), whatever followed is missing. But it is written on the same kind of now-yellowed, blank "Cheney State College" paper, and in Inge's same quick handwriting as a draft of another poem dated 1983:

In this, the final hour of our planet earth.
I feel constrained by haste and worry to give birth
To a few thoughts. On evening news
We analyze the power struggles of the day.
In Lebanon the Druse, the Syrians, the [illegible] say
That the "peace keeping forces" and the Israelis fight
Each for its own end, each for a selfish claim to right.
And in the meantime every day, the various factions.
The occupiers and the occupied everywhere go about zealously
Killing each other in vengeful spite.
Lebanon is but a microcosm of what defines itself
In Asia, Africa, Europe, America, every day.
As Arnold says in "Dover Beach," ours is a place
"Where ignorant armies clash by night." But
Are they ignorant? Surely the ones in the trenches are,
Fighting a war hyped up by
Power brokers who may not be in the know,
Who see their ends as paramount, [illegible]

Even in these personal thoughts about the state of the world, Inge referenced a classic work of literature: the last line of 19th-century poet Matthew Arnold's "Dover Beach." How deeply classical literature was integrated into her thinking!

After Ronald Reagan won the 1984 Presidential election, she wrote to her old friend Charlotte: "What can one say? It is incredible, the proportion of victory, and I'm sure Mr. Reagan will interpret this as a mandate to go full sail ahead ... Foreign policy, the environment, the poor — are all in great trouble." She also wrote of her concern about possible conflict with the USSR, and "stirrings of the poor in Central and South America and South Africa, crushed under cruel dictatorships." She questioned that "our country should swing so inexorably to the right?"

Community papers often heard —and printed — Inge's concerns. To the editor of the *Cheney Record*, the college newspaper, she wrote of her anxiety about a soccer coach who, according to an article in the *Daily Local News*, had been "given his 'walking papers' because he had written an article critical of Cheney, [claiming] that the soccer team was not getting enough support from the students.'" I do not know if this coach's complaint was valid or if other facts contributed to his firing, but Inge's letter bluntly questioned one issue: whether this coach's "academic freedom and/or his right of free speech [had been] violated." That's what mattered to Inge.

After the terrorist bombing of Pan-American Airlines Flight 103, two legal scholars proposed, in a *New York Times* op-ed piece, that President George H. W. Bush should repeal American prohibition of political assassination. Their rationale: the threat of retaliation by legal political assassination would deter terrorists from attacking Americans. Incensed by this recommendation, Inge wrote a letter in response. (See next page.)

On August 17, 1991, Inge was disturbed by President George H. W. Bush's comment on the Democratic party's opposition to his "no-domestic-policy." She spoke her mind to the *New York Times*. Subtlety in this letter was not one of her writing tools. (See next page.)

Letters

What's Still Wrong With Political Assassination

To the Editor:

In arguing that the United States should repeal its public prohibition of political assassinations ("Repeal Order 12333, Legalize 007," Op-Ed, Jan. 26), David Newman and Bruce Bueno de Mesquita assert that opposition to assassinations on moral grounds is "weak" since "Virtually all societies recognize the right to take another life in self-defense." Just when did self-defense motivate an assassination? And when did everybody's doing it morally justify an immoral action, not that the attempt to do so isn't made every day?

The pragmatic justification the authors use rests on the equally shopworn, highly popular belief that only force or the threat of force begets the submission of the adversary. More than 3,000 years of recorded bloodshed do not, I think, definitively either sustain or refute this argument, for peace still eludes both the strong and the weak.   INGE PROBSTEIN
Lansdowne, Pa., Jan. 28, 1989

"Just when did self-defense motivate
an assassination?"
Inge asked.

A Domestic Policy Is Coming Soon

To the Editor:

You quote President Bush in a Kennebunkport, Me., news conference on the Democratic opposition: "I think they've come upon a theme. Go after the President on no-domestic-policy. And I will be retaliating at the proper time" (news article, Aug. 17).

While it's hardly news that political strategy is in the saddle, I am startled that lack of a domestic policy can be dismissed as a theme, that we may get a domestic policy only "at the proper time" and that this policy will come only as retaliation in a political contest.

In the same article, you quote both President Bush and Senator Bob Dole as concerned about possible backlash against the Operation Rescue demonstrators in Wichita, Kan., not about the group's denying others access to what is still a legal medical procedure. Once more, the concern is tactical, not the defense of rights.

Clearly, what we need in this country is a re-education in values, rather than in strategies, and from the top down.   INGE PROBSTEIN
Lansdowne, Pa., Aug. 17, 1991

"I'm startled that we may
get a domestic policy
only at 'the proper time.'"

122

In 1987 she wrote to Supreme Court Justice Harry Blackmun in response to the Supreme Court's *Maryland v. Garrison* decision. In that case, the police found drugs and cash in an apartment they had mistakenly raided. They had a warrant to raid the third-floor apartment at an address, but they didn't know the third floor had two apartments. They inadvertently raided the wrong one, and in it found items that violated Maryland's Controlled Substances Act. The tenant of the raided apartment, Mr. Garrison, was ultimately convicted. Justice Blackmun (and Justices Brennan and Marshall) dissented, based on the Fourth Amendment's rights against unreasonable search and seizure without a specific warrant. Inge agreed with Justice Blackmun and registered her disagreement with the court's decision. He responded with a personal note:

Supreme Court of the United States
Washington, D. C. 20543

CHAMBERS OF
JUSTICE HARRY A. BLACKMUN

March 4, 1987

Ms. Inge Probstein
65 Bryn Mawr Avenue
Lansdowne, Pennsylvania 19050

Dear Ms. Probstein:

Thank you very much for your letter of February 25 concerning <u>Maryland</u> v. <u>Garrison</u> and the dissenting opinion. The Court did not go along, but that is the way the system works. It helps to receive letters such as yours.

Sincerely,

Harry A. Blackmun

PART TWO

INGE:

MY TEACHER, MY FRIEND

That is part of the beauty of all literature. You discover that your longings are universal longings, that you're not lonely and isolated from anyone. You belong.
F. Scott Fitzgerald

The mediocre teacher tells. The good teacher explains.
The superior teacher demonstrates. The great teacher inspires.
William Arthur Ward

CHAPTER 24

CREUTZBURG

In the spring of 1984, newly retired and well-rested after the frustrations of her last years of teaching, Inge knew what she wanted to do: she wanted to go back to school — to sit on the other side of the desk. At 62, she wanted to be a student again. Life was comfortable. She continued to share a house with her mother and with, as always, a beloved cat. Hans, her brother, came on weekends, usually leaving her irritated. But she enjoyed day trips and going to concerts with friends, and finally she had the time and opportunity to indulge her enthusiasm for exploring her many interests. That led her to the Creutzburg Center, an adult education school in nearby Radnor, PA, where she enrolled in a French Civilization course, and anticipated taking cooking and painting courses as well.

It was a fortuitous step. When the director of Creutzburg learned of Inge's credentials and expertise, she asked Inge if she'd be interested in teaching a literature course; the syllabus would be Inge's choice. Inge shocked herself by accepting the offer. She thought all her teaching days were only in the rearview mirror, but she couldn't quell this offer to re-ignite her passion and share it in a new kind of environment. It spurred an unexpected opportunity to look ahead, to plan again. That's how Inge's Creutzburg career began.

And that's I came to know Inge. I had been a high school English teacher, always looking to satisfy an unquenchable pleasure in literature. I knew nothing about the teacher of the course called "Three Who Shaped Modern Drama," but the title attracted me. It was fall semester of 1984 when Inge offered her first Creutzburg course.

That negative attitude toward teaching, which had depressed her in recent years and encouraged her to retire, took a total reversal. In a letter to a friend about her new Creutzburg position, she wrote, "My class was lively as ever ... They are not entirely taken by Chekhov, but unlike my [former] students when they don't like an author, these people want to read more and more of him — they always wish to read more plays than I'd planned to teach, which is just fine. What they miss in Chekhov is the sort of crisis-mentality that suffuses all of Ibsen's social-concern plays that we've been reading for five weeks. At any rate, I can't tell you how fine it is to have a class where people have read, have read well, are 99% present every time, wish to learn, think, get involved. It was a stroke of luck for me to get this experience, for I had really lost faith in the point of teaching anything, lost faith in 'education.'"

The retired professor had finally found professional fulfillment. She was teaching students whose interests in literature swelled with every session. Inge's Creutzburg class started with about ten students meeting in a second-floor, former bedroom of the Creutzburg Center, a stately old mansion, but it increased every semester until a waiting list had to be formed. Then the administration moved the class downstairs to the former parlor in the converted 1880, Frank Furness-designed, summer home of Judge John Hare (1816 - 1905). Still, no more than 25 seats could be crammed into the classroom. Chairs lined the four walls of the rectangular room, so everyone faced the center as well as each other, ignoring the bookcases and fireplace behind one row of chairs, and the several French doors that opened onto a wrap-around porch behind two other rows. The porch looked out over the estate's 30-acre park, which was purchased by the township in 1969 for Main Line School Night, an adult-education program. Despite the name of the program, Creutzburg Center, named for a founder of the program, soon began holding classes day *and* night. Inge held class every Tuesday morning from 9:30 to 11:00. Semester after semester many of her students re-enrolled, showing up with filled-out registration cards in hand as Creutzburg's doors opened on the first day of each semester's enrollment.

Inge's teaching reputation attracted a cross-section of the community with a variety of curious minds seeking to expand their learning through literature. Among the repeating students were a museum specialist in Egypt and Mesopotamia, two social workers, several homemakers, a psychiatrist, a radiologist, teachers (elementary school, high school and college), artists, a lawyer, an advertising executive, a nuclear engineer, two non-college degree participants, two scientists and some business retirees. It was not surprising that a good-natured, gifted literature teacher leading inquisitive students seeking challenging world literature could create a successful class. But this class was more than successful — thanks to Inge. It was her brilliance, warmth, humor, and personality that ignited a spirited chemistry that connected these classmates.

The Harford Mansion in Harford Park, Radnor, Pennsylvania.
Originally the home of Judge John Hare, this Frank Furness-designed house
is now The Creutzburg Center. photo credit: mainlineneighbors.com

CHAPTER 25

CHOOSING THE SYLLABUS

At the end of almost every semester, the class somewhat democratically
decided on the reading for the next semester. Inge offered a few alterna-
tives, and the class voted. Some possibilities, for example: (1) Victorian
novel: Dickens, Hardy, Trollope; (2) Renaissance studies: Machiavelli,
Erasmus, Montaigne; (3) Chaucer: Canterbury Tales.

Several semesters in a row, Chaucer's *Canterbury Tales* appeared on
Inge's list. And every semester Chaucer lost. But one year Inge announced
that she had made an "executive decision": she was overriding our democratic process. Chaucer's *Canterbury Tales* would be the next semester's
literature. No one smiled at this announcement, but no one dropped out.
Inge made us fellow travelers with The Nun's Priest, The Reeve, The Friar,
The Miller, and the Wife of Bath, etc., and at the end of the semester, a
unanimous vote claimed it had been one of our best semesters.

Sometimes Inge put the syllabus on hold, such as after the study
of *To The Lighthouse.* Enamored with Virginia Wolff, the class accepted
Inge's suggestion to spend a week on supplementary readings, i.e., *A
Room of One's Own*, Lytton Strachey's *Eminent Victorians*, and/or Leon
Edel's Bloomsbury, *A House of Lions.*

In 2000, a classmate compiled a three-page list of the authors and
literature Inge had taught at Creutzburg since 1984.

Al's design work

What we have read from 1984 through 2000

Russian Literature

Leo Tolstoy
1828-1910
- War And Peace
- Anna Karenina
- The Death of Ivan Ilyich & other short stories

Fyodor Dostoyevsky
1821-1881
- The Brothers Karamazov
- Notes From the Underground
- Crime and Punishment

Ivan Turgenev
1818-1883
- Fathers and Sons
- A Hunter's Sketches (short stories)

Anton Chekov
1860-1904
- Five Plays
- Short Stories: The Lady with a Dog

German Literature

Johann Goethe
1749-1832
- Faust

Thomas Mann
1875-1955
- Buddenbrooks
- Death in Venice
- The Magic Mountain

Heirick von Kleist
1777-1811
- Michael Kolhaas

Herman Hesse
1877-1962
- Steppenwolf

Franz Kafka
(Czech, but wrote in German)
1883-1924
- The Trial
- Metamorphasis
- Short Stories

Italian Literature

Dante Alighieri
1265-1321
- The Divine Comedy - Inferno

Niccolo Machiavelli
1469-1527
- The Prince

Italo Calvino
1923-1985
- Marcovaldo
- Numbers in the Dark: Short Stories

French Literature

Michel de Montaigne
1533-1592
- Essays

Moliere
1622-1673
- Tartuffe and other Plays

Stendahl
1783-1842
- The Red and the Black

1

*Three pages of authors and titles studied between 1984 and 2000,
categorized by authors' nationalities*

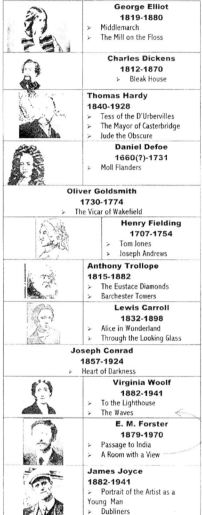

French Literature (continued)

Honore de Balzac
1799-1850
- Pere Goriot
- Eugenie Grandet
- Cousin Bette

Gustave Flaubert
1821-1880
- Madam Bovary
- A Sentimental Education

Emile Zola
1840-1902
Germinal
L'Assoumoir

English Literature

Geoffrey Chaucer
1343(?)-1400
- Canterbury Tales

Christopher Marlowe
1564-1593
- Dr. Faustus

Jonathan Swift
1667-1745
- Gulliver's Travels

Samuel Johnson
1709-1784
- Rassalas

Jane Austen
1775-1817
- Emma

William Blake
1757-1827
- Selected Poems

Charlotte Bronte
1816-1855
- Villette

Emily Bronte
1818-1848
- Wuthering Heights

George Elliot
1819-1880
- Middlemarch
- The Mill on the Floss

Charles Dickens
1812-1870
- Bleak House

Thomas Hardy
1840-1928
- Tess of the D'Urbervilles
- The Mayor of Casterbridge
- Jude the Obscure

Daniel Defoe
1660(?)-1731
- Moll Flanders

Oliver Goldsmith
1730-1774
- The Vicar of Wakefield

Henry Fielding
1707-1754
- Tom Jones
- Joseph Andrews

Anthony Trollope
1815-1882
- The Eustace Diamonds
- Barchester Towers

Lewis Carroll
1832-1898
- Alice in Wonderland
- Through the Looking Glass

Joseph Conrad
1857-1924
- Heart of Darkness

Virginia Woolf
1882-1941
- To the Lighthouse
- The Waves

E. M. Forster
1879-1970
- Passage to India
- A Room with a View

James Joyce
1882-1941
- Portrait of the Artist as a Young Man
- Dubliners

2

132

American Literature	
	Nathaniel Hawthorne **1804-1864** ➤ Selected Short Stories
	Edgar Allen Poe **1809-1849** ➤ Selected Short Stories
	Herman Melville **1819-1891** ➤ Selected Short Stories
	Henry Thoreau **1817-1862** ➤ Walden
	Mark Twain **1835-1910** ➤ Huckleberry Finn
	Henry James **1843-1916** ➤ Selected Short Stories ➤ The Portrait of a Lady ➤ The Bostonians ➤ What Maisie Knew
	Edith Wharton **1862-1937** ➤ The House of Mirth

Upton Sinclair
1878-1968
➤ The jungle

Theodore Dreiser
1871-1945
➤ Sister Carrie

	Ralph Ellison **1914-1994** ➤ The Invisible Man

Spanish Literature

South American Short Stories
➤ — The Eye of the Heart

	Jorge Borges **1899-1986** ➤ Labyrinths (short stories)
	Isabel Allende **1942 →** ➤ The Stories of Eva Luna
	Miguel de Cervantes **1547-1616** ➤ Don Quixote
	Gabriel Garcia Marquez **1928 →** ➤ One hudred Years of Solitude

Miscellaneous Literature

Desiderius Erasmus
1466 (?)- 1536
➤ Praise of Folly

	Henrik Ibsen **1828-1906** ➤ Plays
	Bertolt Brecht **1898-1956** ➤ Plays

Ryunosuke Akutagawa
1892-1927
➤ Rashomon and Other Stories

	Naguib Mahfouz **1911 →** ➤ Palace Walk
	Isaac Bashevis Singer **1904 – 1991** ➤ Gimpel the Fool

Short Story Anthologies
➤ Points of View
➤ Modern European Short Stories
➤ Short Shorts

3

CHAPTER 26

THE NATURE OF THE CLASS: AN EXAMPLE
(THE SERIOUS AND THE HUMOROUS)

Our class was like fine wine: age was a vital ingredient. The youngest students were 40-something; the oldest, 80-something. While some were there to study the literature they had never studied before, others were there to study *again* the literature they had read long ago. No academic credit. No exams. No seeking to further a career. And no pressure to prepare for class. We all enjoyed the pleasure of literature stretching our minds, and everyone appreciated sharing the rewards that Inge's keen intelligence and low-key leadership stimulated. Inge, with her closely cropped gray hair complementing her down-to-earth demeanor, comfortable in corduroy slacks and a crew-neck sweater, knew no pretension. She was a calm leader and a shrewd observer of human nature. She was the spark that ignited our class with boundless literary spirit.

In the fall semester of 1989, every Tuesday morning retired nuclear engineer Al Arker subjected himself to the rigors of Hell. So did social worker Stephanie Tashjian, retired math and philosophy teacher Irene Ryan, art history connoisseur Rilice Lefton, and semi-retired lawyer Miles Kirkpatrick — a few of my classmates enrolled in Inge's course on Dante's *The Divine Comedy*, Part I, "Inferno," the 14th-century Italian poet's allegorical trip through the underworld.

In the vivid imagery of *Hell*, Virgil leads Dante down a treacherous spiral path, past increasingly painful levels of unspeakably tortured sinners. At each level, Dante is intended to gain further understanding. In a sense, Inge was our Virgil, guiding us, week after week — on a distinctively more pleasurable trip — into deeper and deeper understanding of Dante's theme, forms of evil. Though written over 700 years ago, the poem initiated endless contemporary insights, at time making this work increasingly distressful. But Inge's lead certainly enlightened each step with appropriate historical, religious, and political insights. Inge, the conductor, started class with challenging questions on the assigned reading, appropriate anecdotes or stimulating commentary, and kept class discussion moving ahead on track. Despite her own seemingly insatiable knowledge, she always encouraged appropriate "soloists" among the classmates.

Dante would not have been as clear without Irene Ryan's expertise on the theological framework of this literary Hell and on the papacy of the Middle Ages. Dante would not have been as dynamic without Al Arker's insights on concepts which biblical Christian dogma developed into a physical Heaven and Hell. Dante would not have been as appealing without Italian language teacher Ester Ceravolo's bell-toned readings of the original Italian or of the nuances she felt were missing in the translated English text. And Dante would not have been as graphic without Rilice Lefton's slide presentation of the 19th-century French artist Dore's *Inferno* illustrations. In this class, Hell was a deeply rewarding experience.

In her subtle manner, Inge stimulated the class to think independently and critically. She wanted to hear everyone's thoughts — usually significant, sometimes inconsequential. And everyone else wanted to hear them too. Early in the study of Stendhal's *The Red and the Black*, Al Arker had noticed certain similarities between the protagonist, Julien Sorel, and the biblical figure Joseph. He had observed that each of these two significantly different literary characters had served in another's household, had been intimidated by older brothers, and had employers whose wives were infatuated with them. This unexpected comparison initiated unforeseen insights — some professional, some prosaic, but all welcomed. In all the years of Inge's Creutzburg classes, there was never a shortage of contributions or of Inge's encouragement of them.

After studying Dante, every once in a while in subsequent semesters, someone would suggest, rhetorically, into which circle of Dante's Hell a character in a totally different book presently under discussion might hypothetically land. Once this class delved into a book — absorbed it, enjoyed it, "owned" it — that book "belonged" to the class, and mention of it might naturally pop up in discussions of other literature as well as in pre-class casual conversations about contemporary life.

Not only did mention of characters from one semester's book sometimes infiltrate discussion about books in subsequent semesters, but Inge's dry humor often transposed recently scrutinized literary characters into funny, end-of-semester "updates." She'd withdraw them from their proper pages and instill them into the day's current events, labelling her closing-day creations *"Where Are They Now?"*

Even those not familiar with the literary characters could still enjoy Inge's ingenuity, keeping in mind that the class had spent months studying these literary figures with sincere, serious, critical analysis. Inge must have had as much fun writing these "updates" as the class had hearing them. Of course, to fully appreciate Inge's deadpan humor, knowledge of both the literature and that year's contemporary politics helps. The following are from early 1990's semesters. Anyone familiar with the characters and events in these classics — Thomas Mann's *Buddenbrooks* and *The Magic Mountain*, Stendhal's T*he Red and the Black,* and Balzac's *Pere Goriot* — will especially appreciate Inge's "Where Are They Now?" updates:

"Hanno's friend Kai, the famous author, is currently in hiding at Ida Jungmann's house for abandoned cats in Scotland. Under

the pen name of Salman Rushdie, Kai last year published a novel cruelly satirizing the Protestant ministry. Pastor Tiburtius is suing him in Riga."

"Madame Vaquer runs a successful bed-and-breakfast in Manhattan, known as the Helmsley Palace."

"Goriot's daughters, Anastasia and Delphine ... have, in contrition, joined Mother Theresa's mission in Calcutta. [Three Magic Mountain characters] are guests at the mission, working on the movie script for the revue "Oh! Calcutta!" Christian hopes to star in the production after he completes his cure at the Betty Ford Clinic in California."

"While the Buddenbrooks firm continues to flourish as Brooks Brothers, the Hagenstroms are under a cloud because of unsavory manipulations in Texas S & L's. They have fled to Cuernavaca, Mexico, where, in addition to three hotels, they own a Taco factory. Sic transit Gloria mundi."

Our class loved Inge's shift from serious literature professor to humorous character manipulator, a range in personality that reflected her professional expertise, her insights into everyday news, and her down-to-earth charm -- the charisma that kept us stimulated week after week, semester after semester.

During all those years in her class, we were not aware of her family tragedies, her personal challenges, and her devastating depressions. Despite inordinately painful history, Inge seemed to exemplify the philosopher Ludwig Wittgenstein's claim: "Humor is not a mood, but a way of looking at the world." Fortunately, she relished applying humor to the cornerstone of her life — literature. After a semester seriously immersed in Cervantes' Don Quixote and his cohorts, Inge's end-of-semester "Where Are They Now?" included:

"Don Quixote has succeeded Lee Iaccoca as head of Chrysler, now Chrysler-Mitsubishi, after he invented the windmill-driven car. All Chrysler-Mitsubishi cars come equipped with a statue of Dulcinea Telboso on the hood and a howitzer in the rear to deter tailgaters and other enchanters."

"Sancho Panza, ever the realist, has gone into agribusiness in North Carolina. He runs a five-million-acre fig-leaf plantation for Senator Jesse Helms, now head of the International Arts foundation."

"Sancho's wife, another realist, operates a shoe store on Manhattan's Fifth Avenue with Imelda Marcos."

"Rocinante, the Don's horse, won the triple crown at the Derby, at Pimlico, and at Belmont last year, all at a very fast trot. Sancho's mount will join the Borax 20 Mule Team at Devon in May."

Following a semester in American literature, Inge's "Where Are They Now?" informed us: "I am happy to report that many of the characters in the stories we have read are alive and well among us."

"Brother and sister of The House of Usher were ingeniously restored to life by Dr. Jack Kevorkian, who is practicing in reverse now. Unfortunately, their house is still a wreck …"

"Mrs. Hutchinson of 'The Lottery' was not stoned to death after all. Kafka's jackals from 'Arabs and Jackals* rushed in in the nick of time and bit all the stone-faced villagers in the ankle. This distraction allowed Mrs. Hutchinson to escape to New Jersey, where she serves with distinction as Commissioner of Gambling.

*Kafka is from a different semester.

138

After one semester, Inge summed up our studies in "*Tuesday Morn-ings at Creutzburg Center*"

We have sounded Faust and Faustus,
Gone with Dante straight through Hell,
Climbed with Thomas Mann the mountain —
It was tedious, truth to tell.
Buddenbrooks we thought less enervating,
Middlemarch more penetrating,
To the Lighthouse quite sublime.
Though Jane Austen kept us waiting
Often for a long, long time,
Dickens rushed us, breathless, through
His transmogrifying stew.

How we wept through Balzac, Stendhal!
Machiavelli taught us all.
(Now we know why Mr. Quayle
*Chose at Murphy Brown to rail.)**
And Erasmus, that great wit,
Said we're fools. We're sure of it.

How we loved Tolstoy and Chekhov
And "The Lady With the Dog"!
Dostoevsky was distressing;
All his people went Magog,
Not to mention Kafka's Gregor,
Changed to metamorphic smog.
Prompting our profound impressions
In our Tuesday morning sessions,
These and other works have led us
To an overwhelming question:

Smells of goulash used to waft up
From cooking class below;
Of course, we asked ourselves
"Can we hold out til lunch — or no?"

*1992 VP candidate Quayle condemned the sitcom because an unmarried star gave birth.

"A Few Thoughts on Creativity"

Inevitably, anecdotal comments sometimes took us off course. Although Inge welcomed a variety of insights and opinions, she never let us go too far afield, always returning our focus to the assigned literature — its themes, character development, settings, writing style, tone, creativity, and its creator.

The creator was a popular subject of discussion. Readers usually like knowing about writers, and the topic was a fair one, as long as we recognized the author as subject is different from the book as subject. Influences on authors and their personal motivations, including psychological incentives, often captured the class' interest. I do not recall Inge's specific views on that subject, but years later, reading her collected essays, I learned that she was well informed about Freudian theories, including those on the arts. In a one-page, undated, rough copy of a paper entitled "A Few Thoughts on Creativity," she specifically addressed the issue of creators of aesthetic arts. The essay is her reaction to Sigmund Freud's "Creative Writing and Day-dreaming" and Otto Rank's "Der Kunstler" ("The Artist").

"The important contribution of Freud and his followers to aesthetics," Inge wrote, "was to show that the entire human being in his unconscious as well as in his conscious drives is involved in artistic creation and that 'meaning' in a work of art may reside in symbolic forms whose significance may be hidden both to the artist and to the beholder."

Continuing, she added "So far so good." But then she questioned their theory that creative drives result from, or displace, suppressed primary drives. "The shortcoming, as I see it," she explained, "… is that the psychoanalyst concerns himself with the manifestations of the patient's subconscious conflicts, fears, desires, etc., so in his aesthetics he concerns himself with the psychic origins of the work of art, its interpretation as related to these psychic origins." I understand these words to mean Inge considered this approach too narrow, suggesting it's a contrived approach — that is, it avoids appreciating the actual components of a work of art — the aesthetics. What about the paint-er's purposeful choice of lines and shapes and color? What about the writer's purposeful choice of specific words to create meaning and effect? Inge's question: "Is every work of art an expression of the artist's suppressed psyche?"

Related to that concern was her objection to university literature courses which spent "50 minutes lecturing on the author's life to every 10 minutes examining the work itself." Facetiously she asked, "Did Dostoevsky write *The Brothers Karamozov* because of his gambling debts? Did Wordsworth have a French mistress whom he abandoned when she was pregnant? Why did Toulouse-Lautrec frequent brothels?" Flippantly, she continued mocking the analysts' additional steps in seeking the "hidden meanings" in a work of art itself, as if one would "establish Kafka's meaning by counting the number of sexually sig-nificant objects mentioned on each page of text: pencils, umbrellas, dishes, etc.

"Though this is rather laughable," she wrote, "it is not so far removed from Freud's own discovery that *Hamlet* is a great drama *because* it deals with the Oedipus complex … it is ironic, at least to me, to note that Freud in his essay on '*The Moses of Michaelangelo*' confesses he must find a *rational* explanation for any work that moves him aesthetically.

"Why?" Inge asked.

CHAPTER 27

INGE AND CLASSMATES: A SPECIAL BOND

In January 1990, during the two-month winter break between semesters, Inge wrote to me, responding to my earlier mention to her that I'd like to write a feature article about our long-standing class (it was only six years old then) for a local newspaper. She responded with enthusiasm.

"I miss our Tuesday group ... , "our 'feast of reason and the flow of soul.'

"(Who said that? 18th c., I think.) I think the secret of success in our group, and of adult education in general, is simply that 'we are all learners. It's our common quest for understanding the text, ourselves, each other, 'what is.'"Then she added, "we certainly learn as much from each other as from whatever work is before us ... The people in our group have so much to give out ... We often get a very rich brew, a heady interchange of opinion." In another note she modestly claimed, "I just happen to be the anchorman of sorts."Teaching this group "is a liberating experience, something one does for its own sake, not for the sake of getting the students to pass an exam or the course. And one has no problem with student motivation because if they weren't motivated, they wouldn't be there. Simple."

It was not "Simple" at all. Inge was giving her honest response, but she was modest to the point of self-deprecating. Clearly, Inge was the reason we kept coming back, semester after semester — even if the syllabus was not our first choice. Inge was the catalyst who created a crew of literature lovers challenged by her coaching and rewarded by her intellect, her character, and our own camaraderie. No wonder no one willingly dropped out.

Who Were These Classmates?

I knew my classmates well — well, at least as well as one can know them through sharing a literature class once a week, year after year after year. But I was curious to know why each of us repeatedly re-enrolled. A questionnaire passed among my classmates brought these responses:

"She offers the enrichment of an avid reader and shrewd observer of human nature and world affairs ... she charms with a wry, puckish sense of humor that engages and relaxes ... She has the subtle ability to make everyone feel he is an important member of the group, contributing to her personal education by their insights."

"Inge has an irreverent reverence of the literature we read. She's loose, and I find it conducive to thinking and reading in different directions."

"Inge draws us in as we all probe together ... Our cultural, geographic, and religious experiences spill over into our highly verbal interpretations ... We don't always agree, but we always leave thinking — and perhaps a little broader of mind."

"This class is therapeutic. I may not feel good in the morning, but by the time I leave here, I feel great!"

Jokingly one student declared she had to explain to friends and relatives her reasons for repeatedly re-registering: "My neighbors think I'm a slow learner! My grandchildren, in fourth grade, are tired of school already. They wonder if they'll have to keep going as long as I do!"

"Normally I come to class with my own interpretation of the reading … Rarely have I come away without a deeper insight, broader interpretations, a variety of viewpoints, and sometimes with a reversal of my position … [This is] because of the caliber of the class … [and] because of Inge's ability to bring everyone into the discussion."

We students, (mostly) senior citizens old enough and experienced enough to appreciate the value of adult education, recognized that George Elliot's *Middlemarch* read at 60 is not the same experience as George Elliot's *Middlemarch* read at 16. All, including Inge — perhaps *especially* Inge — appreciated the lifetime expertise that age and experience contributed to class discussion.

When a lawyer knowledgeable about the English court system announced he'd have to be away for the two weeks Dickens' *Bleak House* was on the syllabus, Inge changed the order of assignments, assuring we'd read Dickens when that lawyer could offer insights into English law. In discussing the Victorian period, prior to reading Jane Austen, Inge often requested a class expert on British history: "Please correct me if I'm wrong." Our native Italian classmate, whose knowledge gave the class the gift of Dante in Italian so we could hear its original rhythm, remarked, "I took the Dante course because I was curious to observe reactions to, and interpretations of, this work by adult American students." Her conclusion: "Admirable it was — the way the challenge was met. Only minds of that caliber could have interpreted Dante's masterpiece as beautifully." A nice compliment from this classmate, but I believe Inge was the energized hub and we students were the spokes she so expertly prompted and propelled.

One year, Inge suggested to a class member, a psychoanalyst, that he teach James Joyce. He responded to Inge in a letter, part of which reads:

"… your course is the perfect place to examine it [he does not state which Joyce book] … The group is one of the most exciting I have ever encountered in its diversity of backgrounds and breadth of interests, its tenacity in pursuing ideas and, most especially its devotion to you. Thus it seems quite obvious that if anyone is going to teach anything in that course it must be you, else the reflection from the sunlight bouncing off all those empty seats will be blinding. The group comes for you, Inge. We can all read for ourselves, but you provide something for us which we could never provide for ourselves. That, among other reasons, is why you are so thoroughly loved.

"Granted that of late it has been fashionable to interpret literature in terms of the sexual preoccupations of a Victorian Viennese neurologist whose practice was too small to keep him usefully employed. And, indeed, some of those interpretations might actually have some truth value, but what the book says to the individual reader ought reflect many other things aside from Freud (religion, language and nationalism for instance, if we respect what Joyce himself felt ensnared the soul). If you are teaching the course, it will do so … Actually you would do a marvelous job."

No one ever wanted to miss Tuesday morning's class, and no one usually did. The respect of Inge's students for Inge, and her respect for each student, combined with everyone's love of the literature and their anticipation for sharing it each week, created a Tuesday morning commitment engraved in each classmate's schedule. Whatever the topic, time always ran out before discussion did, leaving classmates and Inge still conferring even as they left the classroom and meandered together out to their cars. The class might have been labeled "Appreciating Literature and Other Lovers of Literature."

Perhaps Inge's literature class could be described as a dinner party hosted by a gourmet chef who invited her guests to contribute their own special side dishes. She prepared the main course, but nearly everyone around the table added some distinctive seasonings. And everyone at the table savored the results.

In February, 1998, when I was on vacation in Florida, my head was still in Creutzburg. Trying to keep up with Inge's assignments in *Crime and Punishment*, I was inspired by her own fun rhymes to write the following to a classmate:

> Raskolnikov and his acquaintances are here along
>   with me,
> But on the course or on the courts, they are
>   an anomaly.
> So following golf or some tennis sets, I return to my
>   Russian friend
> And try to get inside his head — which I'm not sure
>   I recommend.
>
> Life in Florida is much too quiet, too relaxed for a
>   complex soul.
> Raskolnikov can't bear this pace; he requires
>   some rigamarole.
> Still I hope to keep up with class assignments,
>   in spite of no-pressure days.
> It's just that Dostoevsky didn't write for a reader
>   stretched out on a chaise.

I'd really be grateful if you'd take the time to e-mail
    the pages assigned,
So when I return to real life next month, I won't be
    three weeks behind.
How I hate to miss those class discussions to which I
    look forward every week.
Reading alone can never provide an adequate,
    in-depth critique.
Hello to all classmates — and to Inge, of course. I'll
    miss her insights on what you read.
The way I see it — that *she's* teaching this course
    means Dostoevsky is lucky indeed!

CHAPTER 28

LAST DAY OF THE SEMESTER

A last-class, informal luncheon marked the end of most semesters. We tried to create a light buffet menu that reflected the cultures of the literature we had just studied. For instance, after analyzing and enjoying Thomas Mann's *Buddenbrooks*, we had a German buffet, for which Inge, an excellent cook and baker, volunteered homemade pickled herring and Kuchen, a sweet German cake. Following the study of Virginia Wolff's *To The Lighthouse*, Inge commented, in tribute to the class' enthusiasm, "I'm so scared of this class that last night at 9:00 I looked up how to make Boeuf en Daube," the French stew keystone of Mrs. Ramsey's famous dinner party in that Virginia Wolff book.

As serious as Inge was in discussing characters' motivations, cultural influences, or any number of profound, significant themes in a novel, she always gave vent to her sense of humor, her inclination towards playfulness — especially on the last day of class. Serious study was her natural persona, but humor lay ready to surface. Even way back in her Yale graduate school days, when she wrote the scholarly thesis on *Boswell's London Journal*, she had also chosen to write that paper on appreciating Lewis Carroll's "nonsense for nonsense's sake." Now, decades later, Inge enjoyed contributing bits of "nonsense" to our celebrating the last day of serious class study. Sometimes, instead of "*Where Are They Now?*" character updates, she wrote limericks about the authors we had so earnestly studied. She prefaced the following with "a ditty on the French 19th century novel to the tune of 'Brush up your Shakespeare' in *Kiss Me, Kate*":

Brush up on Zola!
Start reading the rest!
Digesting his thirty-some novels
You'll be several degrees past depressed.

Brush up on Flaubert!
His style will restore you to glee,
And what does it really matter
If he too damns the French bourgeoisie?

Brush up on Balzac!
His hundred-some volumes detail
That the greedy, the nasty, the shifty
Are the ones who too often prevail.

The novel, a middle-class passion,
Abounds with such churls in its zoo,
And with ladies so loose in their fashion
That they'd rather seek love than cook stew;

With class-strife that's lacking compassion
And all 'family values' askew,
We may ask of these novels we've read,
Just what under heaven is new?'

In response to Inge's creative little ditties, at the end of the semester in May '89, the class presented to Inge our own rhyming lines, along with a monetary gift:

150

After Marlowe and Goethe we tried to read Hesse.
Our minds were confused, but now they're a messe!
Just kidding, Inge, we all loved the course.
Your knowledge and insight were a splendid resource.

With new fictional friends we are certainly blessed —
Good and bad souls suffering terminal unrest.
Faustus and Haller — two of a kind,
Analyzing themselves right out of their mind.

Mephistopheles and Lucifer, Hermine and Job —
What a mixed bag of characters cavorting the globe!
They've all become pals, close buddies of ours.
How they ruled us each Tuesday with soul-stirring powers!

So a summertime break is appropriate now
To read *The Trial*, perhaps, or something lowbrow.
Inge, we thank you; we're all a bit wiser.
You're a great teacher and leader — and a devilish advisor!

Please use this gift well. There's just one stipulation:
Don't buy into a deal with smooth-talking Satan.
Keep well and keep fit. Keep your humor intact.
We'll meet in the fall. We can't wait to come back.

The "nonsense" rapport between Inge and the class grew into an end-of-semester tradition. After 11 weeks of rewarding but serious, analytical insights, we all looked forward to lightening up our literary load with rewarding but lively, illogical inanity. In 1991, we expressed our enthusiasm for Inge with this little rhyme of thanks:

Inge, dear Inge, so bright and able,
Conducting class at Hans Castorp's table.*

151

Joining with Mann are Conrad and Kafka,
A trio of students on our behalfka.

In their land of fiction, these three overheard
That you'd taught a class on their printed word.
And your students' discussions spanned the Bible to Freud —
No subject in the world did that class avoid!

Now Conrad nor Kafka, not even Mann
Had sensed the deep meanings their works had taken on.
The three came to meet you, to finally know
The real depths of their writings they'd penned long ago.

Though the dining room door kept slamming quite loudly*
The authors paid heed to you, Inge, most proudly,
For they knew you were special — informed and refined —
More than Naphta, Settembrini, and Berghof combined.*

Conrad ate little (he really craved ivory),
While Kafka's eye caught something crawly and connivery.
Mann just enjoyed all the food served for thought —
(Five meals a day never made him distraught).

In their days, these three authors knew successes and strife,
But today they are grateful, for you gave them new life.
Yet, not nearly as grateful as we, whom you took
Every Tuesday a.m., deeply into each book.

Inge, dear Inge, you're so sharp and clever.
We'd like you to teach us forever and ever.
Whomever we study, whatever we read,
We want to keep learning — with you in the lead.

*Referring to characters and situations in Mann's *The Magic Mountain*.

CHAPTER 29

INGE'S SUMMER CAMP.

THE CLASS' "MINI-REBELLION"

In June, following each year's standard two semesters, our class lamented the wait until September for Inge's next course. The summer hiatus was too long a break for us, and Inge felt the same way. So "Inge's Summer Camp," a once-a-summer "feed and read" session, became an annual event held at a student's home.

Unlike our regular semester classes, for which we were assigned about 100 pages, for one of our summer sessions Inge requested a different format. Each of us would plan a no-longer-than-five-minute creative contribution derived from one of these books we had studied: *Buddenbrooks*, *The Red and the Black*, and *Pere Goriot*. She offered some suggestions:

1. *Summarize an alternative to the last chapter — your own creation. (How else might the book have ended?)*
2. *Suggest the direction the sequel might take. (What directions might the remaining characters' lives take?)*
3. *Assume the perspective of any of the characters we've come to know and love (or hate) ... and tell us how you (as this character) really feel towards the other characters ... or how you feel about the author's treatment of you.*

153

4. *If the characters in these books have universal qualities,*
    "who" might they be in today's world? Or what might be a
    comparable situation in contemporary life?

With these suggestions, Inge inspired our creative writing genes, which we'd not recognized in each other — or perhaps in ourselves. Whereas Inge's "*Where Are They Now?*" pieces had taken characters out of classic works and facetiously deposited them in contemporary life, this assignment encouraged us to create serious, alternative lives for the literary characters we knew so well. We were daring to confront — or at least co-write with — Mann, Stendhal and Balzac! What a fun afternoon!

Even in a relaxed "summer camp" session, alongside an informal lunch, Inge offered intellectual nourishment that never quite quenched our ravenous appetites.

As I remember, the format of all the other "Inge Summer Camps" reflected our regular classes, along with a potluck lunch. The invitation to one summer session at the home of a student with a swimming pool read: "Option: Bring a bathing suit if you'd like to swim before, after, or during (??) class." Inge was the only one who complied; after class she enjoyed an afternoon of smooth, relaxing laps. She was 79 years old. At that time, of course, we students had no knowledge of her superior swimming skills 60 years earlier, when she was a star on the Agnes Scott College swimming team.

Keeping up with Inge's end-of-semester nonsense poems and her humorous *Where Are They Now?* "updates" of literary characters, our class assumed her upbeat tone in this invitation we created for one summer's "Inge's Summer Camp" session:

> How many classics have you read this summer?
> Or are those intentions in tatters?
> Well, Chekhov's calling you, my friend —
> Time to return to literature that matters.

Another insight into Russians of culture —
That's what THE SEA GULL recounts.
Trigorin, Medvedenko, Shamrayov and Sorin —
Plus a few others we cannot pronounce.

We'll discuss the play on July the sixteenth
After salad and desserts at noon.
(Perhaps Counselor Inge will regale us again
With her Russian literature lampoon!)

If you plan to enroll in Inge's Summer Camp
Please reply by July the first.
See directions enclosed. From wherever you live,
You'll just have to drive a few versts.

Class "Mini-Rebellion"

When Creutzburg's increasing number of courses outnumbered available classrooms in the converted mansion, Creutzburg administrators assumed Inge's devoted students wouldn't care where the class met. They were wrong. They moved us to Bolingbroke, a colonial mansion about a mile from Creutzburg, with rooms for large gatherings and events. But Bolingbroke was also being used as a nursery school. Running and jumping little feet plus shouting and laughing little children were not conducive to serious literature discussion. Our class rebelled.

In a "DECLARATION OF DEPENDENCE," calligraphed by a classmate on a colonial-type, tan parchment scroll, we wrote to the Directors of the Creutzburg Center:

DECLARATION
OF
DEPENDENCE

When in the course of the Creutzburg Center, classes outnumbered classrooms, and it became necessary to ask Our (Inge Probstein's) Established Literature Class to dissolve its well-founded ties and move to a separate and unequal building, We accepted the Creutzburg decree that impelled our separation. And we spent this semester enduring patient sufferance.

But now, a decent respect to Our Opinions requires that the Creutzburg Board consider our request (nay, our plea) to return to a Proper Classroom at The Creutzburg Center next semester.

Prudence, indeed, will dictate that classes long established (more than eight years for most of us) should not be changed if the new environment precludes academic Life, intellectual Liberty, and the Pursuit of Education.

Though Bolingbroke seems to lend itself to the Safety and Happiness of older adults seriously in search of informed literary understanding, wee children marching on our heads as well as additional inexcludable (no door!) distractions, are decidedly injurious, unwholesome, and unbearable.

We appeal to Your Native Justice and Magnanimity. We are Loyal Students who continue to enjoy the tie that created and bound This Class to This Center. We function well here because we are dependent on a Proper Classroom Environment. Through years of Resolute Re-enrollment and Attendance, we believe We have Earned our Right to a decent classroom.

SO ...

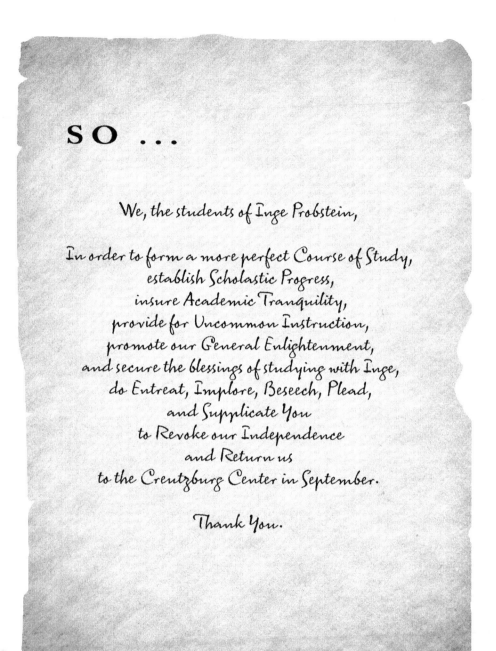

We, the students of Inge Probstein,

In order to form a more perfect Course of Study,
establish Scholastic Progress,
insure Academic Tranquility,
provide for Uncommon Instruction,
promote our General Enlightenment,
and secure the blessings of studying with Inge,
do Entreat, Implore, Beseech, Plead,
and Supplicate You
to Revoke our Independence
and Return us
to the Creutzburg Center in September.

Thank You.

The following semester we were back "home" in our big, light, airy, quiet, 1880's parlor of the Creutzburg Center.

CHAPTER 30

THE STROKE. THE CLASS WITHOUT INGE

On a Sunday in May, 2002, Thelma and Irwin Bessen, classmates who lived near Inge and often kept in touch with her between Tuesday classes, called her several times. No answer. On Monday they tried again. No answer.

At this time, Inge had been living alone with a beloved cat for years. Amelie's physical and mental health had seriously deteriorated in her old age, and Inge had deplored having to send her to a care-giving facility, where she died at 98 in 1986.. Hans remained a resident of Haverford State Hospital until he died. I do not know the date of his death, but it was before this institution closed in 1998.

The Bessens, concerned that Inge hadn't answered her phone in two days, went to her house, and through the window they saw her lying on the floor.

Word of Inge's stroke stunned our Creutzburg class the next morning. Although the doctors wouldn't, or couldn't, yet predict the long-term results, we learned that Inge was as shocked as we were that she was in the hospital. She had no memory of what had happened to her. When she recovered enough to have company, a group of her devoted students visited her in the hospital, and on June 11, 2002, we took some balloons and a cake to her bedside at Bryn Mawr Rehabilitation Center to celebrate her 80th birthday. "That was the best birthday of my life," she claimed later.

In the various rehab centers of assisted-living facilities in which Inge lived after her stroke, she worked diligently with therapists to regain physical competence; she did reclaim her ability to walk, at times depending on a walker to assure balance. In all my visits to her, she never complained. In fact, she often noted the good meals she had been served as well as the helpfulness of the staff. And she readily praised the facility's cultural programs she had attended or planned to attend. If a sign-up sheet on a bulletin board advertised a concert or a speaker or an outing to a museum or store, Inge registered. She was a frequent visitor to the Center's library, and she painted in the arts-and-crafts room almost daily. All the nurses and aides became her friends, and she initiated amenable relationships with all those residents who were lucid enough to respond.

But it seemed clear to me that Inge was becoming increasingly passive. I did not know if the stroke had reduced her thinking capacity or if the lack of challenging mental stimulation in rehabs and assisted-living facilities had weakened her ability to express herself. She was still an active reader, but her handwriting was steadily deteriorating, reflecting significant motor control changes. As time passed, both her speaking and writing acuity declined, with German words and phrases slipping into her writing, and syntax sometimes resembling a new immigrant's struggle to translate into English. Eventually, Inge's scratchy scrawl, often illegible, suggested a quiet prisoner, sadly restrained, but determined to keep trying to escape.

In her first writing after the stroke, she recalled the calamity. "I've had all sorts of adventures since I had a stroke. First there was only the antithetical consciousness of my attitude. I can remember getting a space-maker [sic], and, in the first days of my stroke, the two nuns who helped me at Sacred Heart [Hospital]." And she recounted vivid dreams she had while hospitalized, many taking place in Germany.

Meanwhile, despite our class' heartfelt hopes for Inge's full recovery, by July her obvious condition warned us that she would not be able to teach in September. Though we could never replace her, we refused to disband. We were addicted to our Tuesday morning meetings. So when the Creutzburg administration advised they had no one to substitute for her, we held an emergency summer meeting and decided to start the search ourselves.

An email to the English Department of the University of Pennsylvania, describing our class' long history with Inge and our past courses of study, brought two responses. One was from Michael Vitez, a *Philadelphia Inquirer* feature writer who taught a non-fiction class at Penn. In his response, he noted "I can't offer to teach your class, because I'm sadly deficient in the works of literature. I read your email and wanted to TAKE your class, not teach it." His real reason for responding: "I'm always looking for good stories to tell. It amazes me that your group has been together, largely unchanged, for 18 years. That is incredible."

The second response was from Robert Regan, a recently retired English professor, who could commit to only half a semester, six weeks. That worked well though because Martha Goppelt, the recently retired head of the English Department of Agnes Irwin School, a nearby private girls' school, was willing to assume the other six weeks. Their shared commitment lasted several years.

Michael Vitez, the *Inquirer* reporter, followed through on his interest in Inge and our class. In the fall semester, he came to class for our second post-Inge session, Bob Regan's class, and asked to join me after that class on my visit to our beloved teacher. Inge, Michael and I sat in a gazebo on the rehab grounds. In Vitez' subsequent *Philadelphia Inquirer* article, he wrote: "When talking about her class, [Inge] became sharp and passionate.

"'It was to me eternal,'" Inge murmured. "'If I hadn't had this stroke, I suppose I'd be teaching it.'" Asked if she missed teaching, "Inge broke into tears. 'It's terrible to give it up,'" she whispered. Vitez' article claimed that I, too, had tears in my eyes.

Inge's memoir notes that when she moved to Bryn Mawr Terrace, another assisted-living facility, she felt she had "started to live in ... 'Freiheit [freedom],'" where she spent much of her leisure time painting. "The physical therapy department was eager to help, and taught me the stairs to negotiate. They were helpful also to turn on the music in a head phone to listen in." When she was "promoted to the third floor ... everything was fine. I remember the table mates. And a coffee hour. I got a scotch to drink and I danced freely before all the guests ... Of particular mention ... here I met ... [a woman] and her mother, so reminiscent of my own mother."

In October 2002, I visited Inge at Bryn Mawr Terrace on a Tuesday morning after our Creutzburg class. She was her normal, post-stroke self: subdued, passive, serious, but glad to have company. Expecting my visit, she was waiting for me inside the main entrance. I didn't know if she'd want to talk about our class or if that would make her sad, but after a few moments of "how are you?" and "how are you adjusting to being here?" and "do you feel you are making progress?" I didn't know what else to discuss. Inge seemed almost withdrawn, so I told her about the subject of that morning's Creutzburg class, the classic *Mont St. Michel and Chartres* by Henry Adams. The author, though not that specific book, clicked with Inge. She told me she had read Adams' *The Education of Henry Adams* twice, and she'd loved it, adding that only parts of it remained with her. I had read *The Education* many years earlier, and was sure whatever Inge remembered was definitely more than I did. But I was relieved to find a topic we could share. Now, in retrospect, I wonder at the coincidentally appropriate mention of the educator/historian Henry Adams. One of his most quoted lines is "A teacher affects eternity; he can never tell where his influence stops." That quotation did not come into our conversation that day, but now I reflect on how accurately it revealed our relationship.

Inge wanted to talk about the theme of Adams' autobiographical *The Education*. In essence, it's about his being educated for a successful future in the dominant culture of the time (a church-driven culture), and then finding himself an adult in a world with a changed dominant culture (an industry-driven culture). I was thrilled that in conversation Inge seemed more like her pre-stroke self. But in just a few minutes, she was only vaguely focused, and I sensed she did not really care about the subject but was merely being polite.

Then, out of the blue, Inge startled me. "Demuth expresses a similar situation," she announced.

"What! Where did that come from?" I asked myself, almost aloud. "Charles Demuth? The American painter? How did he get into this conversation?" Inge unknowingly answered my unspoken question. Evidently she had been studying Demuth reproductions, for she reached to a nearby table to pick up a book of his work. Methodically she turned the pages to point out the characteristics of his completely different styles, quietly commenting that his subject matter and style were inspired by different cultures at different times in his life: early on, the Pennsylvania Academy of Fine Arts instruction that produced his fluid watercolors on paper, with soft colors and enough white to suggest a brush barely touching the paper, and his subject matter sometimes merely a suggestion; and later, Marcel Duchamps' and the Cubists' influence that turned Demuth to an exponent of "precisionism" in oils — geometric and sharply defined shapes, even of bold commercial lettering complementing hard-edged abstractions of buildings.

Inge saw a connection. Like Adams, Demuth had been educated in one culture, and found himself an adult functioning in another. Although Henry Adams (1838-1918) had felt the new dynamo-driven culture had forced him to reject his education and recognize new influences, and Charles Demuth (1883-1935) had made a personal choice to follow the art world's new culture, what Inge had connected was that both men understood and accepted that the world for which each man had been educated had changed, and each acknowledged the power of his new world. In Inge's pre-stroke days, when she was intellectually sharper, drawing this perception might have been just the beginning of deeper insights, a spark with which she would ignite class discussion, leading to thinking beyond the obvious, perhaps recognizing individual experiences that would lead to awareness of universal issues. That she perceived this comparison in her present mental and physical state convinced me that deep down Inge's mind was still in gear.

But just as bluntly as she had blurted her Demuth comment, she abruptly ended the discussion by turning silent. And to me this silence felt palpable. "Quick! What can we talk about?" I pressured myself. I wanted my visit to cheer her, to brighten her spirits, but her reticence, her rail-thin body, her weak voice, and her downcast mouth created a barrier that made me anxious. Desperately I again turned to our common ground, our Creutzburg class.

"Inge, in class this morning we began discussing a possible syllabus for next semester," I said, mentioning that one suggestion was T. S. Eliot's *Four Quartos*.

"Oh, yes!" she replied with a small burst of enthusiasm. "*The Four Quartos* are Eliot's best work. The class should read them for a summer project." Maybe mentioning future semesters was wishful thinking on my part, or maybe it was my desire to give Inge hope, but aware that my words might be unwise, I still let my natural reaction declare, "That might be a class *you'd* like to lead."

"Yes!" she exclaimed, just as impulsively. Then, silence again. Had she suggested putting off Eliot until the summer, skipping the upcoming spring semester, because she knew she wouldn't be up to teaching it yet (if ever)? Had she mentioned "a summer project" because our class usually met in the summer for just one afternoon of lunch and discussion — a very informal session — which she might be able to lead? I didn't know if I had caused her hope or despair.

CHAPTER 31

CROSSLANDS TO BLUE BELL PLACE

Finally, after months of waiting, Inge's application for acceptance at Crosslands arrived. This was the Quaker retirement residence in Kennett Square, PA, where she had always hoped to eventually retire. In January '03, while I was away, she wrote to me in shaky script: "I love it here. As you know, it's a *Magic Mountain* atmosphere [referring to Thomas Mann's book about specific patients in an upscale Swiss sanitorium, which the class had read a few semesters earlier]. I am treated with great kindness (so is everybody else), and I have many friends already."

In the spring, I visited Inge there several times, and each visit was pleasant. Although she never smiled — probably a physical after-effect of her stroke, Inge was as upbeat as could be expected. She exuded pride in showing me the tastefully landscaped grounds, the indoor pool, the art studio, and the wood workshop, where some residents' work was displayed for sale. She was delighted when I bought a beautifully hand-crafted, desk-top wooden book rack which a resident, her friend, had made.

One day she invited me for lunch. We had an elegantly served meal (Cornish hen) in a well-appointed, white-tablecloth-and-fresh-flowers dining room. Clearly Inge was proud of her Crosslands home. Often as we walked through or sat for a while in the residents' lounge area, she would quietly but seriously point out specific people, i.e., a man slouched in a large wing chair. She told me he was Herr Someone(?), her teacher from her school in Germany — about 70 years earlier. I just let the comment pass. What would be the point of questioning or correcting her?

To celebrate her 81st birthday, June 11, 2003, eight of our Creutzburg classmates took Inge out to lunch at a restaurant near Crosslands. It was the kind of warm, sunny, cloudless day that makes you consciously celebrate the beginning of summer, and we all sat around an outdoor table overlooking the gentle green expanse of a scenic golf course. We hoped this "reunion" birthday celebration would spark Inge's natural personality, ignite her dry humor, stimulate her instinctive self-deprecation. But Inge was not Inge. Her face was totally expressionless; she barely said a word. She ate little, and left the table several times to stand at a distance to smoke. She was with us only in body, which was frail and gaunt.

In December that year, she wrote to me, "Everything has worked out beautifully here," explaining she had found the kind of paints she wanted, and Irwin and Thelma Bessen, the couple who had found her lying on the floor after her stroke, now also residents of Crosslands, had brought her brushes. "I've painted up a storm, and you shall get a sample ... I am reading Dr. Johnson's London ...," (Samuel Johnson, the 18th-century literary figure, a subject of her Yale Ph.D thesis on Boswell).

But her long awaited retirement at Crosslands was short-lived. In this smoking-prohibited facility, she had dropped the lit butt of a cigarette in a trash can. I learned of this second-hand, and was not told if there was a fire, but the act of smoking itself crossed a strict Crosslands rule, provoking her expulsion.

In her notes on remembering life at Crosslands, written after she had moved to Blue Bell Place, an assisted-living facility in Norristown, PA, she explained, "It took me so long to recognize my tablemates

Tante Anna and das Mitterlr. Downstairs was Tante Paula ..." [Tantes Anna and Paula were the Essinger sisters from the Kinderheim of Inge's early childhood years.] Ogilvie was here, and so was Frau Winkler, both married to others. I gave mine poetry and mine essay on Freud's 'Aufsatz' [article] to her and she understood."

Still reminiscing about Crosslands, she wrote "In summer I went swimming and in winter I tried to survive in the pool ... I spent money like mad. I bought books from West Chester Bookstore and Barnes & Noble. I bought ... stuffed animals ... I spent money at the Spanish Store." (Crosslands took residents on outings to nearby shopping centers.)

Of her new residence, Blue Bell Place, she wrote, "This place is but all idyllic ... I have all my books. And room so fine ... Painting is easy. The shopping we do is always in Walmart ... I wish I had a cat, and a car, and I wish to have a home, so I could cooking [sic] ..."

These first notes written from Blue Bell Place are significantly revealing. First, they show that though Inge had left Crosslands, her love of that retirement community had deeply impressed her and was lasting; she was still thinking about Crossland residents (including those her deteriorating mind told her were people she knew in Germany) as well as her good experiences there. Second, despite her expulsion from Crosslands, Inge seemed to have easily adapted to Blue Bell Place, noting that though she'd rather "have a home," her new facility was pleasing to her, and she seemed grateful for its services. And third, some of Inge's writing at this time suggests that her mind sometimes slid back as if translating from German into English, as she had to do when she first came to America at 12 years of age. Now, as then, it was not always accurate.

But mostly, Inge was still functioning reasonably well. In February '04, in a note card with a cat on the front, she wrote to me: "The Group [referring to some members of our class] was here yesterday, and I read them some poetry that I wrote in Bryn Mawr Terrace. I cried when they left. Because I would rather be teaching the group. They had lunch in our coffee shop, and they very much liked it ... Excuse my scribble." In the

P.S., she recommended a book to me: Eva Hoffman's non-fiction *After Such Knowledge*, the story of long-term implications of the Holocaust on survivors' children.

I visited Inge every two or three weeks. On one summer visit she met me at the door dressed in pink cotton slacks, a white tee shirt under a pink-trimmed white sweater, and sandals. She still seemed to care about putting herself together. Even so, her lined, dry face, which used to have an earthy, natural glow, was now ashen, sallow. Her wispy, uncombed, stringy gray hair hung loosely about her expressionless face. It would have been easier to remember Inge as a brilliant, sensitive, self-deprecating, funny, retired English professor in whose adult-education class I studied for 18 years. But I felt a commitment and a need to visit her, to look past her turned-down mouth and tired eyes.

CHAPTER 32

HOW I CAME TO TELL INGE'S STORY

One cold, gray autumn day, she was expecting me about 1:00 pm. There she was, waiting at the reception desk, bundled in a turtleneck, overall blue jeans, an unbuttoned trench coat, and a gray knitted wool hat pulled down over her ears. Sometimes she could barely breathe. She'd gasp, cough, wheeze — every strained breath an audible struggle. Her frail shoulders hunched over the walker she wheeled about Blue Bell Place, which now comprised the length and breadth of her outer world. Attached to the walker was a basket holding her basic needs: that day's *New York Times*; *Nora*, an ear-marked paperback about James Joyce's wife; a book about the Revolutionary War's *Battle of Paoli*; and the latest *New Yorker*. Stuffed beneath those necessities were a clump of tissues and a rolled-up, wrinkled jacket. Her inner world was not always discernible. Sometimes it showed determination to deal with daily routines; sometimes it indicated infusions of childhood German flashbacks.

Greeting me with a stiff hug, she suggested we go out to the patio, the only area where she was allowed to smoke. Not snow, nor rain, nor heat, nor gloom could ever keep Inge from this addiction. No matter when I visited her, in mid-sentence or mid-word, every two hours an internal siren sent her scuffling to the nurses' desk to request her precious, allotted cigarette.

"Does a doctor check you?" I asked, following her to the gated patio.

"I use a breathing machine," she mumbled softly, her words slightly slurred.

"How often?" I questioned, concerned about her rasping, repercussive cough.

"Every day. It helps a lot." She fingered the unlit end of her cherished cigarette, then drew on the gratifying nicotine that satisfied her habit, as we sat in a chilly drizzle.

When she extinguished the tiny stub, we went inside and walked through the colonial Williamsburg-styled lounge area and down the bright hallway to her room, a comfortable but cluttered, book-crammed haven. Inge sat on her twin-size bed, the length of which abutted one wall. I looked to the upholstered, three-pillowed sofa across from her bed, but layered as it was with socks, magazines, sweaters, books, and a jumbled quilt, there was not even room for one. I don't think Inge realized that, so I gently pushed aside just enough to make room for me. In front of the sofa a coffee table was all but hidden under a hodge-podge of newspapers, catalogues, books, mail, whole boxes of Whitman's Chocolates as well as loose jellybeans, and copious art tablets of Inge's watercolor work. She was now fully committed to painting as a creative outlet.

I was not surprised at the disarray. It struck me that here in this room was everything — everything except her cigarettes — capable of giving her pleasure. This room was Inge's world. She was surrounded by the accessible objects that mattered to her — her books, her records (from a catalog she had ordered a modern "Victrola"), her watercolors. Orderliness was irrelevant.

Inge sat still, looking down, silent, pensive. It had been months since she had sustained looking directly at me. Not sure what to do or say, I began turning the pages of her watercolor tablets, noticing that the earlier works were groups of figures seated on a sofa, broadly sketched in intense primary colors sometimes separated by Roualt-like black outlining strokes.

"These are residents here, seated in the lobby," she explained. Clearly, they were suggestions of figures seated close together in a row. Were they her friends, or just a subject to be painted? No clue. Inge said no more. As I turned the pages, and moved on to more recently painted tablets, I noticed that the subject was repetitive — figures seated close together in a row. But in the more recent works, the figures were much less specific and the colors were more muddied. I wondered if she had tired of painting the same subject but wasn't motivated enough to consider a different one, so she'd just repeated the same one, but with less attention. Or was diminishing eyesight causing her to see those figures less distinctively? I didn't ask her. She saw me looking at the different versions, but never offered a comment. Then I wondered if she even realized the differences in the subsequent tablets. I think she did, but wasn't up to, or interested in, talking about it. Her mind was somewhere else.

Soon Inge reached over to her night table, just as cluttered as the coffee table, and picked up a thick, overstuffed manila folder crammed with hand-written loose-leaf pages and tablets, many yellowed and fading.

"This," she mumbled, "is my life story."

What? Had I heard her correctly? The importance of the statement and the indistinct muttering of those words just didn't equate. I didn't know if she noticed my raised eyebrows or silent gasp, but she was looking directly at me. Momentarily I saw Inge's eyes brighten and her shoulders straighten. I actually sensed in her just a bit of that vigor that had defined her teaching style, that energy that had motivated our class. I saw the former Inge, the one who brought literary characters to life and who recognized classic literature issues reflected in our contemporary world. This energized change in her demeanor was striking, but brief. Possibly drawing on long-gone confidence, she then declared in a whisper, enunciating as clearly and forcefully as she could, "This story must be told."

At that moment the dimension of our relationship changed. It was clear to me that nothing mattered more to Inge than this mission, and in a responsive burst of caring, loyalty and gratitude to my teacher of 18 years, nothing mattered more to me than helping her fulfill that mission, though I had no idea how.

"Oh, Inge!" I exclaimed, a bit dumbfounded, as I walked over to the bulging packet of papers, and extended my open hand as if to ask, "May I look?" Inge was glad to comply. Perhaps showing me these papers wasn't a spontaneous act on her part; perhaps she had planned this for my visit that day. Stunned by both the existence of her autobiography notes and her clearly articulated declaration of their importance, I spent the next few minutes skimming some pages. In the back of my mind, a very practical thought occurred: I might never again be strained to think of a topic for conversation with Inge when I visit.

The first page, a brief retrospective of the 1930's Nazi Germany political environment of her childhood, preceded keen observations and vivid memories of her sensitive, formative Third Reich years. Despite all my years as her student, I knew none of her life story. Most pages had been handwritten over a period of years, probably in times of good health and humor and vitality. Most of it, but not all, was legible, with occasional words and phrases appearing in German. Some typed pages — mostly lines in poetic format — were faded carbon copies.

"What do you plan to do with this?" I asked her. She said nothing, but looked directly at me, and shrugged weakly, not in a careless response but as if to say, "I wish I knew."

"Well, Inge," I ventured, "nothing can be done with these pages in handwritten form." She nodded in agreement. On my next visit I brought her an electric typewriter, hoping she'd start typing her story. But about two weeks later, the next time I came to see her, she shuffled to the typewriter and apologized in a soft monotone for not being able to use it. I think in her frail state, the electric typewriter, a "new" machine for her, was too physically and technically challenging. So I offered to take a few pages home and start typing.

My next visit to Inge, in December, was to the Norristown hospital,

171

where she had been taken after a fall. She had left a message on my phone telling me she was there.

"Is Inge Probstein's condition serious?" I asked a nurse behind the counter at the nurses' station on my way to Inge's room.

"Are you a relative?" she asked, barely looking up from her paperwork.

"No," I explained, quickly adding, "Inge has no living relatives. I'm an old friend. I received a call from her informing me she was in the hospital."

"I'm sorry," the nurse said. "We can only give patient information to relatives," and she turned her full attention back to the papers on her desk.

On the hospital tray next to Inge's bed, her small radio softly played classical music. Inge told me only that she had hurt her hip, but barely said more, offering no explanation of the seriousness of her injury, the treatment, or the medication. She did not seem to be in pain or even unreasonably uncomfortable. She was just quietly compliant. If this had been a pre-stroke visit — that is, if she had fallen, hurt her hip and been hospitalized before her stroke, and was similarly "comfortable," I think Inge would have enjoyed my visit; she would have delighted in telling some self-deprecating comments about falling, and would have offered some witty insights about the hospital, her doctors, and her care. But I wasn't visiting *that* Inge. Visiting *this* Inge gave me blunt evidence that her wit and wisdom, her nature — the core of her personality — was either muted or gone.

Surprised by my visit, she murmured that she was glad I had come. But very soon she became exceptionally impassive and lay back on her pillows. I decided this was not a time to try to initiate conversation, but to make my visit brief. Maybe she just wanted to rest or get back to the music, or maybe she wanted to turn to her book-marked books or the newspapers on her night table. I told her I was leaving soon for Florida, but as always, I would write. I hugged her as she lay still, and said I'd see her in April. We didn't mention her autobiography notes.

On January 17, '06, I received an email from Blue Bell Place Executive Director Kathie Fox:

"Hi Judy,

I am contacting you because Inge asked me to call you. I left a message on your home phone number but I know that you are in Florida and wasn't sure how long you were spending there. I'm sorry to let you know that Inge started hospice care today, at Blue Bell Place. She is very weak and on oxygen. If you'd like to contact me, please do so. I don't know if there is anyone in the area that may want to see her. Inge told me that you were the only person that she wanted me to contact."

In my call to Kathie, I learned that Inge had an inoperable mass on her lung.

She died two days later.

Because of Kathie's first call, her second one didn't shock me, but it did leave me in tears, not only because I had grown to love Inge, but because I pictured Inge in her last days alone and sick. She had no living relatives, no one to be with her. In my private mourning, I lamented that she had died alone — a woman so beloved by her adult-education students that they'd devoted every Tuesday morning for 18 years to her class. In my private sorrow, I reflected on what a treasure Inge had been to all of us. And I regretted that after her stroke, though groups of us had visited her regularly, as conversation with her had become more and more difficult, group visits had understandably dwindled. Had I not been in Florida when she died, I would have contacted my old classmates to come together to honor and commemorate our beloved teacher. But I was 1100 miles away. There was no funeral, no service. Inge was cremated according to the instructions she had left with her lawyer.

Kathie Fox asked me about Inge's belongings, but I had no answers as to what to do with them. We talked about the objects that filled her room — everything she owned: literature books, records, a Victrola, art books, artwork, paints, a German doll which her father had given her when she was a little girl, old letters, old photos, academic papers from

Yale, journals, essays and other papers, including several attempts to write her memoirs, especially her childhood years. I was already somewhat familiar with the beginning of those memoirs. Kathie gave me the name of Inge's lawyer, who would assume responsibility for her belongings, and asked me to get in touch with him when I returned to Philadelphia.

Blue Bell Place named the sunny sitting area just past Inge's room the "Inge Probstein Living Room," and placed her books in that room's wall of bookshelves. Perhaps Blue Bell Place residents would share the literature Inge loved, the literature that inspired her all her life and through which she inspired grateful students in her 18-year career that began after she retired.

When I returned to Philadelphia, I contacted Inge's lawyer, who asked me to come see him. On the floor of his garage was a carton with all Inge's papers. On a shelf was a small box with Inge's ashes. I gladly loaded the carton into my car, but I had no idea what to do with cremated ashes. My only meaningful thought would be to bury them on the grounds of the Creutzburg Center, the place which had brought Inge 18 years of pleasure, love, respect and reward. But I was told a township law prohibited such a burial. I do not know what the lawyer did with them.

Glancing through her papers, I realized Inge had started to write her memoir many times. That puzzled me. Did she want to give copies to different people? Did she start and re-start writing as an exercise to fill time? Was re-writing her memories a way to reaffirm their existence? Recognizing the declining handwriting in subsequent accounts of those early childhood memories acknowledges Inge's own aging process as well as her unrelenting determination to tell her story. Maybe all those reasons are valid, but what was certain is she didn't want her life story to fade away.

Understandably, she wanted to tell all the chapters of that story — Nazi Germany and its devastating consequences, school and family challenges in America, academic achievements, religious identity, sexual identity, mental and physical health problems, career challenges and disappointments, and — finally, post-career success. What a story it was.

174

Inge, who was motivated and inspired by literature, whose life embraced the stories of literature, knew she had a story to tell.

In Inge's honor, our class planted a tree near the entrance to the Creutzburg Center, where students attending all adult-education classes can read the plaque at the base of the tree as they go up the few steps to their classes:

In Memory of
INGE PROBSTEIN
Beloved Teacher

I am left with a lifetime of lessons from knowing Inge, learning from Inge, caring about Inge, admiring Inge, and loving my remarkable friend — even long after she lived. Inge gave me the most rewarding assignment of my life. She still resonates in my mind. I am still her student.